Table of Contents

Fortunate Families

Fortunate Families

Catholic Families
with
Lesbian Daughters
and
Gay Sons

Mary Ellen Lopata
with
Casey Lopata

TRAFFORD PUBLISHING

Printed in Victoria, Canada

National Library of Canada Cataloguing in Publication Data

Lopata, Mary Ellen, 1944-
        Fortunate families : Catholic families with lesbian daughters and gay sons / written by Mary Ellen Lopata and Casimer Lopata.
Includes bibliographical references.
ISBN 1-4120-1189-2
        I. Lopata, Casimer, 1941- II. Title.
HQ759.9145.L66 2003   306.874   C2003-904723-7

TRAFFORD

This book was published *on-demand* in cooperation with Trafford Publishing.
On-demand publishing is a unique process and service of making a book available for retail sale to the public taking advantage of on-demand manufacturing and Internet marketing.
On-demand publishing includes promotions, retail sales, manufacturing, order fulfilment, accounting and collecting royalties on behalf of the author.

Suite 6E, 2333 Government St., Victoria, B.C. V8T 4P4, CANADA

Phone	250-383-6864	Toll-free	1-888-232-4444 (Canada & US)
Fax	250-383-6804	E-mail	sales@trafford.com
Web site	www.trafford.com	TRAFFORD PUBLISHING IS A DIVISION OF TRAFFORD HOLDINGS LTD.	
Trafford Catalogue #03-1567		www.trafford.com/robots/03-1567.html	

10   9   8   7   6   5   4   3

Dedicated

To our grandchildren Grace, Maxine, Griffin, Caz, Lily, Julius, and Shira and our godson, John David

. . . they are hope for the future.

And to all the gay and lesbian people who have touched our lives

. . . they help us see with our hearts.

Grateful acknowledgement goes to:

All the parents who completed my initial survey, all those who have called on Catholic Gay & Lesbian Family Ministry or attended our days of reflection;

Mary Ann, John, Steve, Florence, Ann, Phil, Len, Molly, S.J., Connie, Stan, Julie and Dick for sharing their stories;

My children, Jim, Andy, Linda and Dan for their generosity and forthrightness of spirit;

My husband, Casey, who knows all the technical "church" answers but always remembers the person;

Luanne Brando for giving fresh eyes to proofreading;

Len Szumiloski and Pat Lindahl for their unending good humor and encouragement;

Karen Rinefierd for her reasoned pastoral insights;

And lastly Rosalie Muschal-Reinhardt who believed I could write this book, who kept the project on track, who told me "this book will be a big help to many parents and their gay and lesbian children" – and never ever let me forget it.

Preface

"Someday, you will know how blessed you are and how special your son is, because he is gay. He will be a special delight and comfort to you." My friend, Mary, spoke these words when I told her my son is gay. That was many years after Jim came out to me and the truth of her comment was becoming a reality in my life, so I thanked her with a hug and tucked her affirming words in my heart.

Years later, as a graduate student studying how having a homosexual child impacts the family, I came upon Walter L. Williams' *The Spirit and the Flesh*. Much of Williams' book focuses on the social position of the "berdache." "Berdache" is a word used by French and English explorers to describe a physiological male who does not fulfill the standard male role in society; one who has a non-masculine character, and is often considered effeminate. However, to many Native Americans the term "berdache" conveys the positive qualities that "two-spirited" persons bring to some Native American tribes. Williams describes how these societies and families appreciate the uniqueness of certain children who exhibit traits of both sexes, and do not force each and every child to conform to established gender roles. When these children are identified, their talents are nurtured, and they grow up to be great assets for the whole tribe. They are seen as having two spirits—masculine and feminine. As adults they often become go-betweens, negotiating and reconciling disputes between males and females in the tribe. In some tribes they are also mediators between this world and the spirit world, and are greatly honored for this important ritual role in the community. According to ethnographer W.W. Hill, a family with such a member "was considered, by themselves and everyone else, as very fortunate."[1]

"Very fortunate!" How different from our own culture which values conformity, and which is so uncomfortable with people who are different. When that difference involves gender roles or has a sexual aspect, our culture often labels such distinctions as "deviant" or "unnatural." We can learn from tribal cultures that appreciate each individual, value each person's talents, characteristics, and skills, and encourage the development of each person's unique qualities for the benefit of the family as well as the good of the whole community.

I thought about my own family. Did we feel "fortunate" to have a homosexual son and brother—a "two-spirited" person—in our family? What about all the other parents of gay sons and lesbian daughters that I knew? Did they consider themselves "fortunate?" Based on my own experience, I suspected that many privately did feel fortunate but they would be intensely uncomfortable, somewhat embarrassed, perhaps even afraid, to let others know that their family was so blessed. If society will not accept the individual who is different, it will surely not understand the family who celebrates that distinction.

Notes

1   Williams, Walter L. (1992) *The Spirit and the Flesh: Sexual Diversity in American Indian Culture.* Boston, Beacon Press, p. 62.

Foreword

Our oldest son, Jim, who is gay, was born into a traditional Catholic family and baptized two weeks later. He went to Mass virtually every Sunday and Holy Day of his life, attended school of religion classes regularly, went on yearly church retreats, sang in the folk choir, and was a leader in the parish teen group. When he went away to college, he continued to attend Mass and be an active part of the university's Catholic community.

As a family, we were active participants in the family life ministry of our parish, forging friendships with other families with similar religious and moral values. For adult role models, our children had a group of moms and dads committed to what they understood to be core gospel values: love of God and love of neighbor. These values were not empty sentiments but lived realities, demonstrated, for example, by supporting the person next door whose spouse was hospitalized, as well as caring for the Vietnamese orphan halfway around the world. We did not just "go to church;" we believed (and still do) that we, as the people of God, *are* the Church, and must work unceasingly to live up to that responsibility.

Many of us had moved from other places around the country and we became a kind of "intentional" extended family, providing the support and comfort we needed as our children negotiated the often difficult, sometimes dangerous, journey to adulthood. In spite of that closeness, it was three long years of feeling alone and isolated before I told my very best friend—who was one of that supportive network of friends—that Jim was gay. My relief was palpable when her reaction was caring and supportive, not at all judgmental, or worse, pitying.

My delay in sharing this news with my best friend may sound contradictory. How close could this supportive community be if I could not share with any of them, even my best friend, this important fact—if I could not reach out to them? We had shared many other family traumas, including divorce, unplanned pregnancies—of both the parents and their teenage, unwed children—premarital sex, drugs, cheating, alcohol abuse, etc., all the landmines of family life. Well, not *all*! Not once was homosexuality raised in that group. Never! Only once was it addressed from the pulpit, and that obliquely, when a courageous priest challenged Anita Bryant's hateful anti-gay rhetoric.[1] But never was it spoken of in our suburban, upstate New York community. I was a willing participant in that silence, a silence that spoke a loud and clear message: homosexuality was something so bad it could not even be talked about.

My vague understanding when Jim came out to us was that the Church said homosexuality was wrong, period. There was no point in asking questions or arguing. I was too ignorant to even know what questions to ask. At the same time, I was confused because the syllogism, "Homosexuality is bad. My son is homosexual. My son is bad," did not work. It made no sense. In my experience, it simply was not true.

Finding sympathy but not much else from our parish priest, eventually I had to look outside my faith community to find the information and support I needed. Desperate for information about this topic no one would talk about, I stole books from the library. I was too embarrassed to have anyone see me check them out. Months later I returned the books—in the night return. It took years to overcome my embarrassment and shame.

I found some comfort at PFLAG (Parents, Families and Friends of Lesbians and Gays)[2] meetings and Dignity[3] services. There was no support at all in my own faith community, until several years after Jim came out, when our parish Pastoral Associate, Sr. Kay Heverin, offered an adult education series entitled "Homophobia and the Church." Behind the scenes I helped organize and publicize the program, never letting on that I had a personal interest. The series consisted of a role-play experience of discrimination, a presentation by a scripture scholar, a presentation on AIDS and talks by a gay man, a lesbian woman and the mom and dad of a gay son—all Catholic. By the end of the series, I knew in my heart that if I really loved and respected my son as I said I did, I could not continue to deny—by my silence—a part of who he is. I could not remain in the parental closet. It was a gradual process, taking nine years in all. Somewhere along the way, I began to realize what a special gift Jim is to me, to our family and the whole Body of Christ—not in spite of, but —because he is gay.

Notes

1   Anita Bryant led the fight to repeal a gay rights law in Dade County, Florida in 1977.

2   PFLAG is an international organization which "promotes the health and well-being of gay, lesbian, bisexual and transgender persons, their families and friends through: support to cope with an adverse society; education to enlighten an ill-informed public; and advocacy, to end discrimination and to secure equal civil rights." (From PLFLAG brochure.)

3   Founded in 1969, Dignity is the nation's oldest and largest organization of gay, lesbian, bisexual and transgender Catholics, families and friends. Dignity works for education and the reform of the Church's teachings and pastoral practices toward sexual minorities and for acceptance of all people as full members of the Church." (From Dignity brochure.)

1

Introduction

Background

1969 marked the end of a decade of social turmoil. Protest—pushing back against authority, outdated traditions and unfair stereotypes—was like adrenaline, energizing multiple sectors of society. Young people led the way challenging the morality of the war in Vietnam. Civil rights activists risked their lives and people rioted in the streets demanding an end to discrimination against black people. Women became aware of the strength and talent they contribute to the mutual good of the human community, which led to a vigorous discussion of sexual norms and gender roles. In this context, I began to think beyond the limits of my sheltered upbringing.

A young mother of four small children, I barely managed to read the daily newspaper, but I do have a vague recollection of reading about the Stonewall Riots—sometimes called the Stonewall Rebellion—in Greenwich Village, New York City. In the early morning hours of June 28, 1969, New York City police raided the Stonewall Bar. Though such raids on gay bars were common in New York City at that time, this one was different. This time police met concerted resistance from the bar patrons, especially the drag queens, who simply refused to be the continuing target of police harassment. Five nights of violent face-offs with the police followed. Gay and lesbian activists had been working for decades for the cause of gay liberation, largely to no avail. The Stonewall Riots and the publicity surrounding that event marked the turning point. Stereotypes fell as gay men and drag queens stood up, held their ground, and fought back.

This was my first real awareness of gay people—or homosexuals as they were then referred to in the media. The whole concept of homosexuality was completely foreign to me. Yet, as I read the newspaper accounts of the riots, I felt sympathy for the gay men who were treated with such contempt by the law. It never crossed my mind, not for a second, that one of my children was gay.

Soon after the riots, the Gay Liberation Front was founded. Later in 1969, *Time* became the first national magazine to devote a cover story to "The Homosexual in America." In 1973, the American Psychiatric Association removed homosexuality from its official manual of mental and emotional disorders. Two years later, the American Psychological Association followed suit. A most significant and critical component of the fledgling political and social movement for recognition and civil rights was that gay men and lesbians began to "come out of the closet," telling family, friends and work associates of their homosexual orientation. When moms and dads, friends, neighbors and people at work and at church began to know real, living, gay people, they had to reexamine the stereotypes by which they had previously identified homosexuals.

Fourteen years after Stonewall, my oldest son, Jim, would tell me he is gay. Parents like me, whose gay sons and lesbian daughters came out to them in the 1970s, 1980s and even the 1990s, grew up in an entirely different social climate from today. Accurate information about homosexuality was in short supply and these parents, myself among them, operated under a whole collection of "unconscious assumptions" about homosexuality and homosexual people. We "knew" certain things about homosexuality, none of which were good.[1] We "knew" that neurotic family patterns cause homosexuality; that acting like a sissy or a tomboy causes people to be gay; that homosexual seduction or a traumatic event with a person of the opposite sex can cause homosexuality; that homosexuality is a mental illness; that homosexuality is a choice; that homosexuality is immoral; that all homosexual people are promiscuous; that gay men and lesbians live lonely, unhappy lives and contribute nothing to society.[2] Virtually all we "knew" was wrong.

Catholic parent survey

Today parents still learn—through subtle and not so subtle cultural clues, as well as through the overt ranting of some political and religious figures—all the stereotypes, and are also told that being gay is somehow anti-family. Parents are not expected to accept a gay child; in fact, the conventional wisdom in some quarters implies that normal, good parents will reject a gay child and/or do all in their power to "convert," "repair," i.e., change, their child's sexual orientation.

Catholic parents are subject to the same homophobic influences with which all people in our society contend. Yet, many parents apparently overcome that bias and come to accept their gay child without abandoning their faith. Researcher George Sabol asked, "Could it be that a strong personal relationship with God or a strong parental bond with a homosexual child enables some parents to go beyond the proscriptions of their religious denomination and come to accept and love their child despite a sexual lifestyle condemned by that religion?"[3] Sabol concluded, "The parent-child bond is powerful enough to overcome any negative influence on attitudes due to the parents' religious beliefs and practices."[4] *Fortunate Families* illustrates that many Catholic parents negotiate this conflict between what they believe the Catholic Church teaches and their lived experience of affirming their gay child as a whole and holy person.

Given the "unconscious assumptions" parents have when their sons and daughters come out to them, parents often—understandably—respond in a way that their gay child experiences as negative. About half of gay and lesbian youth say their parents rejected them because of their homosexual orientation.[5] Because family relations are a critical part of our social framework and because an estimated three to ten percent of the population is predominately homosexually-oriented, it is important to understand as best we can the family dynamic that occurs when a child "comes out" as homosexual to his or her parent(s). Most data concerning parental attitudes toward their gay sons and lesbian daughters are based on research conducted with gay and lesbian persons. The conclusions of such studies, therefore, reflect the perceptions and impressions of the children, which may or may not be an accurate representation of parents' actual feelings and reactions.[6]

Much anecdotal evidence highlights the stories of parents who react in verbally or physically abusive ways, going so far as to throw the homosexual child out of the home or to disown him/her. These children often find refuge in homeless shelters or with friends. Their stories of parental abuse and abandonment are related over and over to any and all who will listen. These parents who, for whatever reasons, cannot tolerate their child being gay, become the perceived norm and their actions often become the model for other hurting and confused parents.

There are other stories, stories of parents who believe what they learned in religion classes and at Mass every Sunday—that God loves everyone, period. These parents struggle with the negative messages from their church—which uses phrases like "objective disorder" and "intrinsic evil" to describe gay people—but, in the end, believe in the goodness of their lesbian daughters and gay sons and embrace the gifts they offer the family and society. Knowing these stories, I decided to pursue a graduate degree in liberal studies that focused on homosexuality and the family. My master's thesis took the form of a survey of Catholic parents with gay children which, in turn, led to this book.

The survey is strictly descriptive, its goal simply to describe the reactions, emotions, concerns and needs of Catholic parents. (See Appendix A for the survey and Appendix B for the complete results.) The anonymous survey was distributed to parents through Catholic organizations involved in gay and lesbian ministry. These organizations include: The National Association of Catholic Diocesan Lesbian and Gay Ministries (NACDLGM), Catholic Gay & Lesbian Family Ministry (CGLFM) in Rochester, New York, Dignity/USA, Catholic Parents Network, and Courage/EnCourage. (See Appendix C for brief descriptions of these groups and other organizations working with parents of lesbian daughters and gay sons.) Courage/EnCourage declined to participate in the survey and thus the voice of more conservative Catholics is lost in this instance. That loss, however, does not negate the responses of over 200 Catholic parents who completed the lengthy questionnaire.

The parents who responded could be described as the "backbone" or the "heartbeat" of the Catholic Church in America. Eighty-eight percent say their religion is extremely or very important to them; 82% attend mass weekly—7% daily; 86% participate in other church activities. Along with the personal stories, the survey results offer a place to begin to understand the experience of Catholic families who have gay or lesbian members. Who are they? What are their feelings, their emotions? What do they know and understand about homosexuality? What role does their faith life play in this experience? How do they understand Catholic teaching? Do they know they are fortunate? Does their Church know?

Why this book?

The short answer is because there is little available that speaks directly and compassionately to and about Catholic moms and dads of gay sons and lesbian daughters. When my son Jim came out to me, he encouraged me to talk to a priest with whom he had already shared this news. Fr. Tom knew our family quite well and I was relieved that I could talk to someone who already knew. That meant I did not even have to say the dreaded word "gay"—or, even more dreaded, "homosexual." When I called Father, I simply said, "Jim told me," and he knew what I meant. What I remember most about my visit with Fr. Tom is him saying that at least Jim "didn't have a terminal illness." I recall being stunned at those words, and perhaps that's the reaction he wanted. I know Father was only trying to put my fears into perspective. However, he didn't have any idea about what I was grappling with. He didn't understand that, indeed, my greatest fear was precisely that I *was* losing my child. Fr. Tom did his pastoral best; it simply wasn't adequate.

I've heard similar stories from other parents who lament with frustration and sadness, "I went to talk to my pastor and he was kind and sympathetic, but had no idea how to be really helpful." As parents' questions surface—especially questions about how the church responds to our gay children—their frustration with inadequate pastoral care increases.

Eventually I found my way to Parents, Families and Friends of Lesbians and Gays (PFLAG).[7] At PFLAG meetings, parents told of their struggles and concerns around having a gay child, but most were also very clear about their love for their gay son or lesbian daughter. Before long, I was able to predict which parents—no matter how distraught initially—would eventually negotiate the difficult journey to understanding, acceptance and affirmation of their gay child. They were the parents who began their story with a declaration of love for their child. Often, the words were uttered through sobs: "I love my child, but I don't know if I can handle this. I don't know if I can ever accept her/him." Sometimes their declaration had a defiant ring to it that meant, "I don't care what anyone else says or thinks, I love my child!" Listening to them, I knew that the stories of gay and lesbian kids being kicked out of their homes, or parents denying their gay child's existence—those stories that made up the "conventional wisdom"—were only a part of the reality, perhaps a small part.

At PFLAG I also found a perception that the institutional Catholic Church is intolerant and homophobic. I was offered a special measure of sympathy at

PFLAG meetings simply because I am Catholic. That, however, was not the church I had personally experienced. My twelve years of Catholic education, while not ignoring the "don'ts," ultimately emphasized God's all-inclusive love, limitless forgiveness, and infinite mercy. I am not the only Catholic parent to have that kind of experience.

I longed for understanding in my spiritual home. My Catholic faith, always an important and integral part of my life, comforts me in times of loss and stress, illuminates the beauty of creation, and provides hope in times of despair. However, while my faith in God never faltered when I learned that Jim is gay, Catholic teaching only added to my confused and bewildered state. On the one hand, I believe my faith played an important and positive role in my reaction to my son's orientation. Not for a moment did I doubt God's love for him. I was taught that God loves everyone, no exceptions. On the other hand, I read church documents that called Jim's orientation "disordered" and insinuated he was somehow morally suspect and carried a heavier moral burden than the rest of us, simply because of his sexual orientation. The implication was that being heterosexual made any person better than my son—or any homosexual person.

The dearth of good, accurate information and sound pastoral resources about homosexuality leaves parents ignorant and misinformed. This exacerbates the pain and alienation of lesbian and gay Catholics, and in subtle ways encourages their parents to reject them. Many parents have told me of the lost years between them and their gay child, years lost in anguished conflict between loving their child and confusion about Catholic teaching on this subject. Many parents have no one to talk with and lack good resources to help them process this newly discovered aspect of their child. They often lose touch with their child, and sometimes are unable to bridge the gap created by ignorance, conflict and alienation. I believe that all churches—not just the Catholic Church—need to take responsibility for this lack of support and education.

As my husband Casey and I became more involved in ministry with gay and lesbian Catholics, we often found ourselves in the company of other Catholic parents with gay children. We met them at PFLAG meetings, after talks we gave at local parishes, at annual days of reflection we hosted, and at Catholic Parents Network retreats. As we talked with these parents, certain questions and concerns surfaced regularly: fears about their lesbian or gay child's physical, emotional and spiritual safety; concerns about family relationships; questions about their beloved church, its teachings and its pastoral response to them and their gay children. *Fortunate Families* is primarily about, and for, Catholic parents of gay sons and lesbian daughters; parents in other religious traditions will also find it relevant and helpful. It will likewise be useful for those who work in pastoral ministry with such families, as well as those who are active in family life, youth, and campus ministries.

About the stories

Stories make up an important part of this book. Stories help us learn about our world, past, present and future, and more importantly, stories help us learn about ourselves, our humanity, and our place in the world. On the other hand, personal stories are often held suspect and judged self-serving. Yet experience, both personal and communal, is one of the four components of traditional, Christian moral discernment. This discernment model, sometimes referred to as the Wesleyan Quadrilateral, maintains that authentic moral decisions are arrived at by reflecting on *Scripture;* on *tradition*, i.e. church teaching; studying the physical and psychological sciences, i.e. *reason*; and considering lived *experience*—personal and communal, contemporary and historical. For Catholics, at least for those growing up before the 2nd Vatican Council, these components were consistently weighted, with tradition valued most, then scripture, then reason, and experience a distant fourth. In fact, we were encouraged to devalue, if not totally discount, our personal experience in relation to moral decisions—the church would tell us what to do, regardless of our circumstances. Since Vatican II, recognition of the importance of our lived experience in relation to our faith journey has re-emerged. After generations of holding our own experience suspect, we have some catching up to do.

Regretfully, the stories related here do not represent a diverse cross section of Catholic families. Rather, they represent the type of parents that responded to my survey. Most of these parents were in their late forties to early sixties when they learned of their child's homosexual orientation, and those sons and daughters were usually in their early adult years (18-30). These are parents whose children are grown and on their own—or on their way to being so. They may be looking forward to—or experiencing anxiety over—impending retirement. Sometimes fears—about forced joblessness or a pregnancy at this time in life—lurk just under their emotional radar. If all is going well, however, parents at this stage of their lives are feeling like they can start focusing on themselves and on each other, perhaps even looking forward to the joys of grandchildren. They look at their young adult children with a sense of relief that finally the overwhelming responsibility of parenthood is diminishing. So, that is the general context in which these narratives flow from the lives of middle-aged white parents.

Some notes about the book

Reflections, observations, and stories from over 200 Catholic parents form the basis of this book. The names of most persons have been changed to protect their privacy. The exceptions are Florence and Steve Balog and their daughters, Ronnie and Evyn, and Mary Ann and John O'Brien and their daughter, Shannon and her partner Dana, and Len and Molly Szumiloski who wanted their names used. Several others asked that only their first names be used. These stories as well as vignettes of gay and lesbian Catholics address particular themes throughout the book, for example: parents' feelings, family relationships, Catholic teaching, and the role of the faith community. In most of these stories the lesbian daughter or gay son is living in a committed relationship. This neither presumes these relationships have an active sexual component, nor that they don't. These stories simply reflect the lived experience of gay and lesbian Catholics and their parents.

When writing of families like these, it is easy to create a whole new—positive—stereotype of gay and lesbian people. Affirming the goodness of our lesbian daughters and gay sons can lead to ignoring their very human foibles and weaknesses. The reader's indulgence is asked in this matter. Until gay and lesbian persons are accepted as whole and healthy as any of us, it is necessary to emphasize those good and positive qualities they bring to our families and our society.

There are related issues that are not in the scope of this book. Neither the book nor the survey it is anchored in address bisexual or transgender persons. Also, this book will not discuss possible differences in the reactions of mothers and fathers to learning a child is gay, nor will it discuss possible tensions within a marriage that may be caused or exacerbated by the news. It has nothing to say about the complex issues for parents and grandparents that attend the situation of adult children who realize they are lesbian or gay after they have married and had children.

While *Fortunate Families* is not about Catholic Church teaching on homosexuality, one chapter is devoted to that teaching because of its relevance to Catholic parents in this situation. Also, because the voices of siblings are so seldom heard, Jim's brothers and sister have graciously recounted their reactions to learning that their brother is gay, and the book also briefly looks at some ways grandparents may respond to this news.

Every effort has been made to use inclusive language, except for verbatim quotes. I hope I have been successful. Finally, a note about the shifting voice of the book: the reader may notice that sometimes I write about "them," i.e., other parents, and sometimes I write about "us" including myself in the thought, feeling, and experience being described. It just felt natural to write that way and I hope it is not confusing to you, the reader.

Fortunate Families tells the stories of Catholic parents—striving to love and serve God by loving and nurturing their child. From the combined experience of over 200 Catholic parents, gleaned from letters, conversations and the survey data, we encounter the depth of their feelings for their lesbian and gay children, we learn how important their religion is to them, and we hear what they need from their church. Perhaps our shared experience can grow into shared understanding that will create new conventional wisdom—wisdom that requires parents everywhere, of any religious tradition, to love, affirm and nurture this unique child, this gay child, who blesses their family. Then, as we pray and journey together, we will all become "fortunate families."

Notes

1   Borhek, Mary V. (1993) *Coming Out to Parents: A Two-Way Survival Guide for Lesbians, and Gay Men and Their Parents*. Cleveland, OH: Pilgrim Press. p. 11.

2   Griffin C., Wirth, M., and Wirth, A (1986) *Beyond Acceptance: Parents of Gays Talk about Their Experiences*. New York: St. Martin's Press. pp. 23-40

3   Sabol, G. (1996) *Gender and Religiosity: Do These Factors Influence Parental Attitudes Toward A Homosexual Daughter or Son?* Dissertation. Loyola College, Maryland. pp. 5-6

4   Sabol, p. 84.

5   Hetrick-Martin Institute. (1987). FACTFILE: Lesbian, Gay and Bisexual Youth. Referencing Remafedi, G., "Male homosexuality: the adolescent's perspective." *Pediatrics*. 79: 326-330

6   Sabol, p. 4.

7   PFLAG is an international organization which "promotes the health and well-being of gay, lesbian, bisexual and transgender persons, their families and friends through: support to cope with an adverse society; education to enlighten an ill-informed public; and advocacy, to end discrimination and to secure equal civil rights."

2

Connie's Story:
"Be true to who you are"

Connie and Stan are Catholic parents of seven children. The love and closeness of their children is evident in Connie's story. Although Connie's passion-
ate voice is the one heard in this story, Stan accepts and deeply loves his gay
son, too. Stan traveled a longer road to acceptance and understanding than his
wife did, and he is not yet ready to publicly articulate the pain—or the joy—
of that journey. Here is Connie's story.

> It was Easter Sunday evening and all the family had left except our
> son, Dean. I was exhausted from all the activity of the last few days
> and was relaxing with a book when our son said, "Mom, I need to
> talk to you."
>
> I flipped through different scenarios in my mind, wondering what
> was coming. It's rarely good news when an adult child says, "I
> need to talk to you."
>
> We sat down facing each other, neither of us saying anything for a
> few minutes. Finally, Dean said, "Mom, I think I might be gay."

I was stunned. There had never been any indication that this might be, never anything I had picked up on, though to tell the truth, it was not something I would ever have considered for any of our children. I asked him why he thought that and he told me he loved another man. It had happened out of nowhere with a man he considered a very good friend and had taken them both by surprise. They were both struggling with the implications of what had happened.

We talked some more, and I finally said to him, "If you are gay, then God created you that way. If you think you might be gay, you need to find out and if you are, you need to be true to that." As I was saying this, and I do feel God gave me the words, I felt anguish like I had never felt before. Fear for him, for the life he would lead, for the people who would hate him, churned in my head. I felt like howling, like baying at the moon. It felt in a way like it must feel when someone you love deeply is given a diagnosis of a terminal illness. I hugged him, loving him more than ever.

Dean and I had always had a good relationship. I enjoyed his company and liked as well as loved him. I would never have expected this son of ours to be gay. He had never shown any signs of homosexuality, certainly never any of the stereotypical things we think of when comments are made about gay people. He is a tall, athletic, good-looking man, one whom people seek out. He is fun to be with, intelligent and caring. People confide in him, since he really tunes into people and is interested in what makes people tick. He is also someone who cares deeply about other people's opinion of him.

That last fact keyed me in to God having created him gay, if indeed he was. Dean would NEVER choose a life-style, a way of being in the world, that would put him on the fringes of society, one of the outcasts in many people's minds. One of the things he told me that night that really broke my heart was "I never expected my life was going to be like this. I always imagined I would meet a woman whom I would love. We'd marry, have kids. That's one of the hardest things for me. I love kids and the thought that I might never have any. . ."

He told his dad the next day. He had already told several of his siblings and told the rest as soon as he could get to visit them, since he wanted to tell each one face to face. All were surprised and all were supportive, though several later said to me that they hoped this was just a stage he was going through, one that he would outgrow. In my heart, I hoped for that too. He asked me not to tell anyone else until he was certain that he was gay and ready to come out himself.

Dean struggled for several years and he has come to realize and accept that he is indeed gay. He has told some of his friends but he is not ready to come out to the world in general.

My Catholic faith is the centerpiece of my life and it is my hope that our children live and practice their faith. I had always hoped that they would remain in the church and find in it the means to live a life close to and pleasing to God. It is very painful to realize that this church may not be a welcoming place to our son, that he may find in it no tools to help him on his journey.

I spoke to several priests in confidence. Our pastor, a very good man, struggled to be supportive but he was not that well versed on the issue. I spoke to another priest who was very helpful. His much beloved nephew had died of AIDS so he had a deeper awareness and empathy about what I was going through. I prayed! Did I ever pray! I think I was even more fearful of our son evading the issue and maybe coming to live a life that was a lie which would destroy him, than I was fearful of him living an openly gay life and all that might entail.

I read many books on homosexuality—one after the other, trying to understand and to find out what was truth and what was stereotype. My ignorance on the issue was enormous. I had had little contact with gay people and knew none well. I had disliked jokes and nasty comments about gays but was uncomfortable about exactly where gay people fit in. I thought they deserved to be treated equally, without discrimination, but still there was discomfort around many of the issues. No more! All it takes is for someone you love to be in danger of discrimination or even physical harm and that clears up fast.

I am still waiting for Dean to give the green light to tell friends and family that he is gay. It really bothers me that his aunts, uncles, cousins and our close friends don't know. I don't like hiding it from people, as though we are ashamed, when in fact, we are not. It will be very freeing to be able to tell my friends and extended family about our son. His siblings have indicated the same sentiments. We feel no shame or embarrassment in having a gay son or brother. He is someone we love and are proud of. He is as God created him.

I still have fears: That he may find no home in the Catholic Church, that he may turn from God in bitterness, that he may lead a lonely life, that people will reject him or be cruel to him, that he may even be in physical danger, that he will never have children and I fear the danger of AIDS.

And I have hopes: That he will be in a committed relationship; that he will lead a happy, productive, good life, contributing to his world in a healthy way; that he will develop a close relationship with God and live in a way pleasing to Him; that he will feel welcome and accepted in the Catholic Church; that he will be safe and that people will see him as he is, not judge him on a single aspect of who he is.

3

Feelings
& First Reactions

His eyes filling with tears, Jim quietly said, "Mom, I'm lonely. I'm lonely for another man." With those words, I learned my oldest son is gay.

It's hard to describe my immediate feelings. In truth, I was not entirely surprised. From his youngest years, Jim seemed somehow vaguely different—different in ways I could describe—a little more sensitive and caring, more interested in spiritual matters than other children I observed—but I could not label, could not put a name to this difference. From time to time, as he grew up, a fleeting thought of his possibly being gay would streak across my mind—quicker than the blink of an eye. But such thoughts were dismissed even before I could acknowledge them—more accurately, they were *suppressed*. Jim's clear and certain words that night made denial impossible. I was shocked—the way you are when you're watching fireworks. You know there will be a loud bang, pop, crack! You're waiting for it, but you're still startled. I think my heart skipped a few beats. After a moment, with a flood of tears, my heartbeat returned.

I know I told Jim that I loved him but my tears distressed him. He had planned so carefully before giving me this news. He said, "I'm sorry, Mom. I didn't want you to cry. I tried to tell you when there was nothing else stressful going on at home." The truth is that there is no good time to give people news they don't want to hear. Jim actually picked as good a time as possible and, more importantly, he chose his words with great care. His words, "I'm lonely," conveyed his feelings, and his reality, in a context I understood. Here was a 19-year-old college student, lonely and longing for companionship, affection, and love. That I could understand. The fact that his longing was for another man did not, in any way, negate his feelings. With that, I began to understand that being gay is not only about sex, it's about love, affection, caring, nurturing, support, good humor and all those qualities we hope are present in any close, healthy and holy relationship.

However rational I may be now, at the time my feelings and thoughts were in chaos. Remember the sheltered historical and social context I grew up in, my unconscious assumptions, and all that I "knew" about homosexuality. Actually, I knew virtually nothing and questions quickly boiled to the surface: How did this happen? Am I, or is Jim's dad, somehow to blame? Is Jim mentally ill? Had he had some kind of traumatic sexual experience as a child? Is he condemned to hell? Did he choose to be homosexual? I was afraid for Jim's physical safety and concerned about discrimination at college and wherever he might work in the future. I was embarrassed and worried that friends and family would reject Jim—and blame me.

Jim returned to college at the end of that Thanksgiving break, leaving me fearful that he had irrevocably changed and had somehow become an entirely different person. When he came home for the Christmas break we had time to be together and I realized with great relief that he hadn't changed at all. Someone was changing. It wasn't Jim . . . it was me.

The description of my own reactions when Jim told me that he is gay reflects the intense and chaotic range of emotions parents often experience. Parents can be so confounded by this news that their child is gay, that they are poor judges of even their own reactions. My survey asked Catholic parents to assess their reactions from positive (supportive, non-judgmental) to negative (non-supportive, judgmental). When they were then asked to describe, as best they could remember, exactly what happened and what was said when their son or daughter came out to them, parents revealed strong conflicting emotions.

Some stories reinforced the parent's self-assessment, and some stories were in sharp contrast to that assessment. For instance, one mother evaluated her initial response to her daughter as "very negative." However, when describing what actually took place, she wrote: "I told her I loved her, and asked if she is sure, and is she happy with her decision. That's what's important." A father who ranked himself "very positive" remembered saying to his son: "It's your life and you have to live with it." These personal assessments and the details of the stories may seem contradictory. However, we don't know what was going on inside that mother who evaluated her initial response as "very negative," and yet had told her daughter she loves her and only wants to know if she was happy. She may have struggled mightily to say such accepting words to her daughter. Her daughter's memory of the event may be entirely different depending on whether she focused on her mother's words, or sensed an underlying internal conflict. What about the dad who ranked himself "very positive," yet remembers telling his son: "It's your life and you have to live with it?" Such a statement might not seem "very positive" to many, though it might have been the very best this dad had to offer at that moment. These are examples of the great—often unconscious—conflict some parents experience between their instinct to protect their child and their internalized negative feeling about homosexuality.

Sometimes an initial reaction can change—from negative to positive or from positive to negative. Theresa, Bob's mom, ranked herself "somewhat supportive," and described the delayed reaction in their family like this:

> I responded pretty well. I wasn't shocked, I had felt something was going on in his life, but was not sure what it was. His father and I told him we loved him. We wanted him to continue coming home and being a part of the family. We did not want any secrets between us, as we were a close family.
>
> The next morning was very different. His father was ready to sell the house and move out of town—he was never going to tell anyone. The bottom line was that we loved our son and his siblings loved him as well. We knew we had to educate ourselves.

When Art's son Larry came out, Art forgot the goodness and talents his son embodied and hurled names at him.

> I was shocked and I abused Larry by calling him names. He left in anger but my wife convinced me to remember his excellent behav-

ior and absolutely wonderful record—several scholarships. After an initial outburst of anger, I suggested that we could have him changed. However, he said, "No, I don't want to try that." The very next day we told him that we loved him and we would do anything we could to help him.

Almost half of the survey respondents believe they reacted "negatively" when learning their child is gay or lesbian. Some of these parents noted their sadness and disappointment, their embarrassment and sense of guilt. Those parents whose reactions fell somewhere between positive and negative seemed most aware of the emotional battle raging inside them. Though feeling devastated, they tried to be supportive. They cried. Some felt hurt that their child had not trusted them enough to tell them sooner. Others, acknowledging their negative reaction, simply insisted that they would always "love the sinner but hate the sin." Barbara, Jason's mom, felt totally unprepared to handle this news. Her reaction flowed from her shock. Barbara says:

> I was in total shock and cried, almost uncontrollably, for many days. I said many things I shouldn't have, but I'm not sure it could have been any other way—I was so unprepared and unsuspecting. I was angry, with Jason, and with God for letting this happen to us. I felt like it must be a mistake, that maybe he had it wrong. I thought we must have had something to do with it. Since our son has always prided himself on not following the crowd, on being a little different, I thought maybe he was just doing this to be different. We never withdrew our love or stopped wanting him to be part—a close part—of the family. It's that we had to process so much and fit the pieces of the puzzle that is Jason back together.

Confusion over our own acknowledged or perceived reactions to a child's coming out is only one of many feelings that sweep over parents in the days after learning their child is gay. This confusion can hang on for weeks, months and sometimes years. Very frequently, however, these first reactions are just that, first reactions. With time, patience, communication, and education, these feelings gradually get sorted out and the relationship between parent and child grows and deepens with love and understanding.

Naming the Feelings

In October 1997 the National Conference of Catholic Bishops' Committee on Marriage and Family published *Always Our Children: A Pastoral Message to Parents of Homosexual Children and Suggestions for Pastoral Ministers.*[1] This document is remarkable in that it verifies and affirms that lesbian and gay persons come from ordinary, faithful, Catholic families. The bishops recognize the emotional pain parents suffer and the spiritual growth that can be experienced through this new challenge in the life of their family. *Always Our Children* makes this evident by acknowledging and affirming the emotions parents experience when they learn a child is lesbian or gay. They begin by admitting that Catholic teaching on homosexuality may be a source of confusion and conflict for parents. They go on to identify various feelings parents may experience: relief, anger, mourning, fear, guilt, shame and loneliness and, lastly, parental protectiveness and pride. It is clear from this list that the bishops did indeed listen to parents and heard their pain and struggle and their love. These were precisely the feelings parents identified in my survey.

Relief

The bishops showed great insight by bracketing the more painful emotions with feelings that emphasize parents' love and concern. They begin by acknowledging that some parents feel relief after experiencing an often-lengthy period of concern for their child. When they finally know what the child is dealing with, a heavy burden is lifted or, more accurately, shared. Then with that loving trust in each other, they can begin building a closer, more honest relationship.

> For years, Julie and Dick suffered rejection by their only son, Rick. He was distant, silent, sometimes sullen. They knew he was unhappy; they feared he was depressed. They were hurt and somewhat depressed themselves. Unable to break through his silence, they were at a loss as to what to do. So they prayed. After years their prayers were answered in a way they would never have suspected—Rick told them he is gay. They assured him of their love and their relationship began to heal—and grow. That was several years ago. When I last saw Julie, she was glowing. Their family had recently dealt with major concerns around Dick's health and the painful dissolution of their daughter's marriage and, through it all,

Rick had been a pillar of strength and good humor. Just the week before, Julie said, Rick and his friends had treated the whole family to a home-cooked, gourmet Easter dinner. Julie said it was the best Easter ever: their son was with them again.

Parental Protectiveness and Pride

The bishops end their list of parental emotions with "parental protectiveness and pride," declaring that parents, in spite of all their fears, may insist to their gay child, "You are always my child; nothing can ever change that. You are also a child of God—gifted and called for a purpose in God's design."[2]

"You are always my child; nothing can ever change that." Those words, in *Always My Children*, bring to mind St. Paul's letter to the Romans (8:38-39)

> For I am certain of this: neither death nor life, nor angels, nor principalities, nothing already in existence and nothing still to come, not any power, nor the heights nor the depths, nor any created thing whatever, will be able to come between us and the love of God, known to us in Christ Jesus our Lord.

Parents image that same love for their children.

Our lesbian daughters and gay sons are "gifted and called for a purpose in God's design." How "gifted," and for what "purpose" is for each person to discern with and through the Holy Spirit. Parents only observe and recognize the giftedness and purpose unfold in the life of their son or daughter.

Fear

In addition to those more positive, less stressful feelings of relief and protectiveness and pride, there are more negative and painful emotions that often threaten to overwhelm parents. Fear tops that list.

> On October 6, 1998, Matthew Shepard, a twenty-year-old college student, was severely beaten and tied to a rail fence in the cold, windswept grazing lands of Wyoming. Six days later, without regaining consciousness, he died. One week after his death, on October 19, four thousand people, mostly gay and lesbian, demonstrated in the streets of Manhattan to protest the hateful murder. Our son, Jim, lived in Manhattan. He called us that evening to tell us about the spontaneous demonstration.

As businesses closed that evening, the numbers of demonstrators rapidly swelled and soon were spilling off the sidewalks and into the busy streets at rush hour. Jim admitted that he'd had a few very anxious moments as the police, on horseback, moved in, forcing the crowd back onto the sidewalks and corralling them on side streets off Fifth Avenue. A hundred people were arrested in the confusion and turmoil. I felt my own anxiety climb as he described the scene, and I wondered why he—a usually sensible and cautious person--would put himself in such a perilous situation.

Then he said something I will never forget: "Mom, I had to be there. Every gay and lesbian person who was at that rally knows what it's like to fear for their life."

From the moment he told me of his sexual orientation, I realized that Jim, just by virtue of being himself, was always in a perilous situation. I feared for his safety. That vague fear usually lurked just beneath the surface of my consciousness. Even when I read of gay bashing, I would not let myself dwell on the real possibility of that ever happening to my son. And Jim, probably out of concern for me, never told me of the verbal abuse and physical threats he had endured. But as Jim spoke that night a week after Matthew Shepard was murdered, I became acutely aware of the fear, the very real threat of danger, that he and gay and lesbian people in this and other countries around the world live with.

More than three-fourths of the parents in the survey say they fear for the safety and well being of their gay sons and lesbian daughters. What specifically do they fear? The vast majority says their greatest concern or fear is the prejudice of society. Many other fears flow from that over-arching fear of prejudice: fear of rejection—rejection of their child and rejection of the parent her/himself; fear that the lesbian daughter or gay son will lose his/her job;[3] concern about family reaction; fear of gay bashing; and worry about the Church's negative attitude toward their homosexual child. Parents also worry that their gay child will have a lonely life and will not have children. They sometimes fear the possibility of suicide, and parents of gay sons, in particular, worry about AIDS.

In the survey, parents reveal a deep concern with the Church's role in their child's well being. Some believe there is prejudice against gay people in the Church. Many sense intolerance, especially from the Vatican and some of their local bishops, and worry that such judgmental attitudes will alienate their gay child from the Church. They believe that the language used in some Catholic documents, such as "objectively disordered" and "intrinsically evil," may indeed influence their child to turn away from God and certainly away from the Church.

Connie, the mother of seven children, (see Chapter 2) the oldest son being gay, best sums up the range of fears common to many Catholic parents. She says,

> I . . .fear that [my son] may find no home in the Catholic Church, that he may turn from God in bitterness, that he may lead a lonely life, that people will reject him or be cruel to him, that he may even be in physical danger, that he will never have children and I fear the danger of AIDS.

Parents who love their children never stop being parents with all the anxiety, care, concern, joy, love and hope that parental love infers. We may have a special level of concern for a daughter's physical safety and be more anxious about a child who is physically or mentally disabled or disadvantaged, dreading that people might shun them. Similarly, we tend to worry more about our gay children—about the prejudice against them ingrained in our society. Recognizing and naming our fears is the first step to making the world a safer place for all our children.

Confusion

Earlier in this section, I considered the confused and contradictory feeling parents might have. They can evaluate an initial reaction one way, perhaps negatively, and then proceed to paint a quite positive picture of what really happened. Parents who have lived through this life-changing event can easily relate to the clash of emotion and intellect that takes place. What we "know" about homosexuality and what we feel for our beloved child are completely at odds. While we utter words of love and comfort to our child, we are racked with anguished questions.

Confusion was also evident in parents' understanding of homosexuality. When asked to describe their understanding of homosexuality when they learned of their child's homosexual orientation, many parents gave answers that were contradictory. For instance, some said that homosexuality is both a choice and genetically determined. Others thought that homosexuality was both genetically determined and unnatural. Most parents simply confessed to ignorance and confusion on the topic. Fortunately, there are many resources today that can bring order and understanding out of that confusion. (See Appendix D for a list of suggested resources.)

Parents also exhibit considerable confusion about Catholic teaching regarding homosexuality. Chapter 7 will discuss more thoroughly what Catholic parents need to know about homosexuality and Catholic teaching that will help clear some of the confusion and quell some of the fear.

Confusion is high on the list of emotions parents contend with because it brings with it a sense of helplessness or powerlessness, which serves to deepen an already intense fear. Parents don't know what to think and often their imaginations—primed by the stereotype society offers—paint the worst possible scenario.

Grief

To those who have not experienced a child coming out, grief may not seem to be a rational reaction to a child's homosexual orientation. However, grief is a quite accurate description of how many parents feel. One parent described her grief like this:

> I didn't understand at the time, but I came to realize I was experiencing grief. Tightness in my chest and stomach and crying at the drop of a hat—for no apparent reason or when hearing a particular song. Loss of sleep. Also, I am active in my parish. When I went to Mass or a meeting, I wondered what people would say or do if they knew. Every homily I related to my son's homosexuality and knew the homily would be different if applied to my son. I felt these Christian principles would not be applied to my son, if they knew. Church was often the hardest place for me to be . . .

About half of the parents in the survey recognized these feelings of grief. These are parents who have not rejected or disowned their gay child, so why would they grieve? Their child hasn't died; they simply have some new information about that child. But it's not that simple. Some parents said, "Nothing changed, yet everything changed." Author Mary Borhek and Methodist pastoral theologian, David K. Switzer both write of the grieving process that parents experience. Switzer talks of the panic, the "disorganization and despair" parents may feel—which all interrelate with an overriding fear. He strongly suggests that these feelings are extended and perhaps magnified by the lack of community support systems for parents during this traumatic time.[4] Borhek recommends that parents and their gay child work through this grief together, noting that this calls for calm objectivity and patience—especially on the part of the gay son or lesbian daughter.[5]

One way to understand this grief is to realize that parents are grieving for their lost expectations of, and hopes for, their children. Over one-third of the survey respondents said they are concerned that their gay child will never have children, and are worried that their gay child will live a lonely life. These parents grieve the life they have imagined for their child—usually a life very much like their own, only better. These kinds of expectations are so much a part of our social conditioning that we are usually unaware of them until we are faced with their loss.

Let me give an example. Several years ago, I was privileged to be present at the birth of my first grandchild. There, in the birthing room, I watched my daughter—whom I had given birth to 29 years earlier—giving birth to her daughter! Basking in the joy of that miracle, I suddenly became aware of my thoughts. I was thinking, "Someday, this little girl will also give birth to a child of her own."

Now, I'm not implying there is anything wrong with that thought. I use this vignette only to illustrate that even those of us who, by virtue of our experience, should know better easily fall under the spell of cultural and societal expectations; there may even be some instinct involved in this seemingly automatic reflex. I may not have had the details worked out, but within minutes of her birth, I had planned my granddaughter's future. When such expectations are so deeply ingrained, it is natural that we grieve when those expectations undergo radical change.[6]

From the instant of birth—even before that today—when parents hear those words, "It's a boy," or "It's a girl," they subconsciously—or consciously—begin planning that child's life. They may not actually envision the beautiful wedding twenty- or thirty-some years down the road, or the husband or wife or the grandchildren—but the plan is forming, indubitably. Current U.S. culture is steeped in the heterosexual model of the nuclear family. This is a society more likely to bend the child to fit society's expectation than to affirm the uniqueness of any given child and help that child find a way to contribute to the good of that society.[7]

Other feelings parents experience—for instance, fear, guilt, shock and anger—are subsets of this grief. To work through and overcome that grief, we need to know our gay child and the goodness he or she embodies for us, our family, our community, our Church and our world. Hundreds of thousands of parents in the United States alone have succeeded in this emotional, intellectual and spiritual labor of love.

Guilt, Shame, Loneliness, Embarrassment and Fear for Oneself

Over one-third of survey respondents felt guilty and, for a while at least, believed they had caused their child's homosexual orientation. In a culture that is permeated with negative stereotypes about homosexual persons, this burden weighs heavily on many parents. That burden is lifted only if and when the parents realize that being gay or lesbian is part of what makes their son or daughter the unique and graced person God intended.

For three years after Jim came out to me, I talked to no one about his sexual orientation except my husband, Casey, and the parish priest I mentioned earlier. Shame, loneliness, embarrassment and fear for myself were the cause as well as the result of that silence. Years later, I was on a panel of parents of gay children. I talked about my love for Jim, about my tears and my long silence after learning he was gay. During the discussion that followed a young gay man challenged me, saying, "If you loved your son, what were the tears about? If you loved your son, why couldn't you even talk about him?" There are no good answers to those questions. The loneliness and isolation are by-products of the shame, embarrassment and the fear we feel—shame that what our culture deems "deviant" has touched our family, embarrassment about our own ignorance, particularly because of the sexual nature of the issue, and fearful that we will be judged "guilty" by association. "What did I do to cause this unspeakable condition?" These are the thoughts and feelings that so often overwhelm parents who do not have access to support and to good, accurate information about homosexuality.

These feelings—shame, loneliness, embarrassment and fear for oneself—have elements in common: all these emotions turn inward, putting a negative focus on ourselves; and these feelings often have the effect of keeping one isolated and away from the very support that would be most helpful. Parents who get stuck in this particular circle of emotions need extra motivation and more accessible support to break out of their isolation and reach out for the resources they need.

Anger and Denial

Anger seems a natural reaction to such an unexpected and distressing event in our lives and is a part of the grieving process. You may be angry with your gay son or lesbian daughter for upsetting your dreams. Angry with God for doing this to your child—your family. Angry with people—perhaps even a spouse—who don't understand. Sometimes even angry with people—also often a spouse—who are too accepting, some who may seem to be "flaunting" their tolerance while you are still struggling with all the emotions enumerated here.

Occasionally the anger is right out there for all to see and hear. Often our gay children are the targets of that anger and can be deeply hurt by it. At times, however, verbalized anger can be a healthy release. Articulating your anger, in a respectful way, to your child, your spouse, or God can help you identify all the other feelings that are raging within you. Once identified those feelings can be examined. Then you can let them go or use them to help you move on to better relationships with all the people you care about. On the other hand, dwelling on that anger—continually bringing up the pain, the disappointment, the shame—will only drive it deeper into your being and eventually it may drive your child away.

There are times when a silent anger indicates denial. Some parents can be in denial until the day they die and they will have missed the wonderful opportunity of knowing and loving their gay child for who she or he is. Other times, the roots of denial are hidden in our own prejudices. I remember a dad who came to PFLAG meetings off and on for the better part of a year. His lesbian daughter, an only child, was an accomplished woman with a good position at a large, multinational corporation, and a faithful Catholic. Each time they came, this well-groomed, intelligent man would sit in the circle, shake his head and say,

"I just don't believe it. I just don't believe it."

After many meetings, with no apparent progress toward accepting his daughter as a lesbian woman, one of the other parents asked him rather bluntly,

"What *exactly* is it you don't believe?"

After stumbling around trying to articulate an answer, he finally said,

"How can she be a lesbian, when she is such beautiful person, so smart, so accomplished, so good to her mother and me?"

There was the answer. He simply could not let go of his preconceived notions about lesbians. He knew a lesbian couldn't be so smart, so accomplished, so good to her parents, in short, "such a good person," as was his daughter. It was easier for him to deny this important part of his daughter than to give up his prejudices and his stereotyped understanding of homosexual people.

Eventually, he was able to see the inconsistency in his logic. No longer was it, "My daughter is good, she can't be lesbian." Now it was, "My daughter is lesbian. Lesbians can be good."

Conclusion

Our parental instinct to protect our children springs into action when we fear for their safety. Once our children reach adulthood, however, there is little we can do except pray for their safety and well being. Sometimes the ability to immediately accept and understand difficult and distressing news is simply a part of our nature and sometimes that acceptance and understanding is predicated on previous experience. My friends, Mary Ann and John, were ready when their daughter came out to them partly because they had done their soul-searching years before when they suspected their older son might be gay. So, when Shannon told them she is lesbian and brought her life partner home to meet mom and dad they were both welcomed with genuine love and acceptance.

Most gay and lesbian people are filled with anxiety about coming out to their parents—even if they have a loving, honest relationship with them. There are instances when parents and their gay children are filled with relief after the coming out event, especially when there has been an unexplained strain in their relationship or a sense of distance where there was once closeness. These parents might have been experiencing a "dis-ease," a discomfort, a feeling that something was troubling their child or that their child was hiding something from them. Once the child came out, the parent felt that an obstacle to understanding and closeness was removed. For example: A friend of mine, a gay man who has been married and divorced twice, finally discovered his true sexual orientation in his forties. When he came out to his father, his dad, a stoic man of few words, simply said, "Does this mean we can go fishing together again?" The distance he'd felt disappeared when his son could be honest with him.

Parents experience a wide range of often-conflicting emotions when they learn of their child's homosexual orientation. Many therapists say that feelings are neither good nor bad, they just are. When faced with stressful and disorienting situations, our feelings can be thrown into turmoil. Recognizing those feelings, sorting them out, discerning where they come from and what they mean are steps on a journey to deeper understanding—understanding of the situation that instigated the feelings and understanding of one's self. Some parents find it helpful to seek counseling as an aid in this quest for understanding. The best part, however, is that we can take *this* journey—painful though it may be at times—with our beloved children. In fact, for much of the way, they will be our guides. One of the gifts our gay children bring to the family is the challenge to know them and ourselves better and to deepen our understanding of our humanness and our place in creation.

Notes

1   USCCB Committee on Marriage and Family. (1997, revised 1998) *Always Our Children, a Pastoral Message to Parents of Homosexual Children and Suggestions for Pastoral Ministers, (AOC)*. A statement of the Bishops' Committee on Marriage and Family of the National Conference of Catholic Bishops, United States Catholic Conference, Washington, D.C.

2   *AOC*, p. 4.

3   As of this writing only (August 2003) only 14 states have legislation protecting the civil rights of gay and lesbian people: California, Connecticut, Hawaii, Maryland, Massachusetts, Minnesota, Nevada, New Hampshire, New Jersey, New Mexico, New York, Rhode Island, Vermont, Wisconsin plus the District of Columbia.

4   Switzer, David K. (1996) *Coming Out As Parents, You and Your Homosexual Child*, Louisville, KY: Westminster, John Knox Press. Pp. 13-25.

5   Borhek, M. V. (1993) *Coming Out to Parents: A Two-Way Survival Guide for Lesbians, and Gay Men and Their Parents*. Cleveland, OH: Pilgrim Press. Pp. 65-88.

6   Today gay men and lesbian women who desire children often do become parents—through a variety of means. Bringing a grandchild home is often, but not always, a doorway to greater acceptance and understanding by parents who are struggling with their son's or daughter's sexual orientation. Children have a way of bringing people together.

7   Blumenfeld, Warren J. (1992) *Homophobia: How We All Pay the Price*. Boston: Beacon Press. Pp. 23-24.

4

Mary Ann's Story: "I know her, I love her"

Mary Ann and John O'Brien have been married for over forty years. They were founding members of, and were leaders in, their suburban parish for many years. They delight in their children and grandchildren. Experience in their extended world of work and family informed their response when their daughter came out to them. Their story underscores how their lesbian daughter and her partner have enlarged their world.

It was Thanksgiving Day. Two of our four children and several family friends gathered around the table for the Great Feast. The telephone rang; I heard the upbeat voice of our daughter, Shannon, wishing us a Happy Thanksgiving. After handing the phone around for Thanksgiving greetings to all, I was back on the line and she announced to me that she had a new love in her life and it was very special. She said, "Guess what is so special about it." I covered every degree of age, race, disability, income and other quirks that I could think of before I said, "Hey! I give up! Why is he so special?" "That's it," she said. "It's not a HE! It's a SHE!"

I took a short, deep breath then said that if she was happy and this was what she wanted, I was delighted and happy for her. She asked, "Are you sure?" I said, "Absolutely." In the bustle of the holiday, it was the next day before I shared the news with her father. John's reaction was similar to mine: a quick look to be sure I was serious, then saying if she was sure, that was fine.

Our daughter is the third of four children, all born in the 1960s, and the only girl. She was an outstanding athlete, and although she didn't date much, she had many male friends and enjoyed school dances—informal and formal.

At college she was the belle of the freshmen set with more men on her doorstep than she could handle. She had several intimate relationships, but they rarely lasted long—some involved men who physically abused her. The breakup always brought with it depression and self-doubt.

After college graduation, she pursued her life's dream of being an actress. At this stage in her life, her relationships with men, though short-lived, grew into friendships which last to this day. It was during this time that she met her beautiful partner . . .a SHE, not a HE!

I was very anxious to meet and get to know Shannon's partner, Dana. We had that opportunity one summer when they lived with us for three months while they perfected their musical act. It was an important and special time. Dana became an integral part of our family—a second daughter. We experienced their love, their kindness, their caring for each other. Our worry about their safety never fades, but we know they are energized in a community where they are loved and accepted.

Even though we were happy for Shannon and Dana, and love them both dearly, we didn't share this "news" with anyone for probably a year! Eventually all were taken into the loop and survived.

At work I put a picture of Shannon and Dana on my desk and happily responded to colleagues' admiring comments on the pair. Tentatively, I began to tell trusted friends in our community; after several "tries" it flowed. At my retirement party, I introduced Shannon and Dana along with my sons and their spouses—and it didn't hurt at all! I believe the toughest part about acknowledging that our daughter was a lesbian was the selfish perception of what our friends and relatives would think and say.

Maybe our daughter's "coming out" was made easier for me because of past experiences. Homosexual men and women were not unfamiliar to us. Two good friends are a lesbian couple, several work colleagues are lesbians, and John has a gay family member. Several years before Shannon came out, we thought one of our sons might be gay. He had introduced us to his friends at college, many of whom were gay, and at one point I asked him if he was homosexual. He responded that he didn't know. I was scared . . .maybe frantic. John and I talked often, trying to resolve my negative feelings. Of course I never considered seeking help and it was six long months before these "talks" took a realistic bent and I realized if our son was his own wonderful self on Tuesday—that would be no different on Wednesday when and if he decided to tell us he was gay. That son, not gay, is now married and has two children. So, when Shannon told me that she is a lesbian, I had already confronted many of the demons that might have interrupted my relationship with my beautiful, talented daughter whom I cherish.

A few years ago Shannon and Dana began what has become an annual summer bash at their lovely old farm situated on a high ridge between two lakes. Their first summer party took place on her father's birthday. Her brothers all came and about fifty friends. Her friends represented every age, race, religion, national origin, dress, hair color and relationship that her father and I could ever have imagined! At sunset there was a bonfire and many played and sang to him and others brought out a huge cake celebrating his special day. We both cried.

On the way home we mused how wonderful it would be if their small community of friends were a reflection of a world where we accepted difference as commonplace and where we loved and accepted each other because of who we are, not what we do and think, and what color we are. It was a beautiful experience.

Shannon and Dana keep in close touch with us. I would change nothing about Shannon. She is who and what she has always been. It just took her—and us—a few years to discover who and what that was! She is open, thoughtful and kind. She has taught us much about relationships, understanding and acceptance. Dana is our beloved "daughter-in-law." Though the Church's thinking on my daughter and her partner is completely out of sync with mine, it pains me less with time. Perhaps it's because I know her and love her—and they do not.

5

Beyond Mom & Dad:
Sisters & Brothers and Grandpas & Grandmas

Although the survey that forms the basis for this book was directed only to parents of lesbian women and gay men, it seems that a book about "fortunate families" should have something to say about other close family members—brothers and sisters and grandparents. The survey indicates that 96% of the families had more than one child, so siblings are an important part of the family picture. Siblings can exhibit many of the emotions that parents do: anger, sadness, isolation, embarrassment, fear, shock, confusion, understanding, acceptance, relief, etc. A sibling can be supportive of the gay brother or lesbian sister and may be a bridge between parents and gay sibling. Or a sibling can be a stumbling block to family understanding and peace.

Sometimes siblings will come to a PFLAG (Parents, Families and Friends of Lesbians and Gays) meeting to talk about their family situation. They ask for suggestions on how to help their parents in their struggle to accept and understand their lesbian or gay sibling. The support of PFLAG and the available resources are often all they need—that and the counsel to encourage their parents to come to PFLAG meetings too. From the parent's perspective, the concerns I hear raised most often have to do with a sibling's disapproval of the gay brother or lesbian sister or anxiety about what or how to tell a younger child about their gay sibling.

When a sibling is disapproving, it's important to listen, being alert for clues that may signal an anxiety about her or his own sexuality. If this is the case, and it's troubling them, parents may suggest professional counseling for that sibling. Other times it may be a matter of helping them keep issues separated. For example, have there been other problems between the siblings: personality clashes or a history of sibling rivalry? Problems can get lumped together under the one that can get the most attention or sympathy. When that happens, often—in the long run—none of the problems receive the attention they need.

When it comes to telling a younger child about his or her gay sibling, the best advice is to give children information that is appropriate for their ages. (See Appendix E.) Even children in the primary grades hear the terms "faggot," "queer," "dyke," and "lezzie," on the school bus and in the cafeteria and school halls. They may not know what these terms mean, but they quickly figure out they are not nice terms. By junior high, these are the pejorative words of choice. If children use these words, they may feel guilty when they learn their brother or sister is gay. If a parent does not talk to siblings about their gay brother or sister, they risk increasing the child's confusion when they do learn. The sibling will also wonder why this was being hidden from them—is this something to be ashamed of? Being silent does not protect a child, but leaves the child open to misinformation or information from unreliable sources. A child is never too young to know she or he belongs to a "fortunate family."

When Jim came out to me, he agreed that I could tell anyone I needed to tell; that is, anyone who could be helpful to me in any way. We also agreed that *he* would tell other family members, and I asked him to tell his dad as soon as possible. He told his dad the next day, which was a blessing for me. Some gay children ask one parent to keep this secret from the other parent. While gay persons may appropriately make such a request based on their knowledge of their own family, I believe this places a great and often unnecessary burden on the secret-keeper. In effect, the child has put that parent in a locked closet. After Jim told his dad, I dropped the matter of telling other family members. I had confidence that Jim would know when the time was right, and this was his news to tell.

Family dynamics are almost always affected when a child comes out. Often siblings feel displaced since so much attention and emotional energy are focused on the lesbian sister or gay brother. In *The Family Heart: A Memoir of When Our Son Came Out*,[1] Robb Forman Dew tells the story of her family's journey to acceptance and affirmation of Stephen, her gay son. In the story, as Dew and her husband become more and more involved in helping other parents and working for equal rights for gay and lesbian people, her younger son, Jack, begins to feel displaced. Dew writes of an incident when Jack had a flat tire, a blowout, on a country road in New England. When Jack calls home to ask for the AAA phone number, Dew begins to berate him for not carrying the AAA card with him. With anger and sadness in his voice, Jack interrupts her, saying,

> You know, I really don't think that there's any place at all for me in our family . . . I almost had a wreck when the tire blew, and you didn't even ask . . . I just don't fit anymore. There's no room for me. Our whole family's focused on just one thing now, and I know it's important. It's important to me, too. But I feel . . . like I don't really have a home anymore.[2]

Jack's pain is so evident in his words. They are for me hard to read, especially because I know one of my children has similar feelings.

Over the years, I have heard bits and pieces of those familial "coming out" events, little snippets about how Jim came out to one sibling or another. As I began working on this book, I decided, with Jim's permission, to ask his brothers and sister to share those remembrances with me. Their stories follow.

Linda's Story

Linda is two and a half years younger than Jim. With the insight and humor that the passing of time can give, she and I both look back to the early and mid '80s and agree that she was a "challenging" teenager. She was often more out there on the edge than most parents would want their daughter to be, but because she was so "with it," I had every confidence that she would be just fine with Jim's news. This is her story:

> I have a clouded memory of how Jim "came out" to me, however I distinctly remember my feelings. Jim dropped many hints, which I conveniently ignored. For example, I figured Jim wanted to go to

a gay bar because he was cool and open to alternative lifestyles. The reckoning that he was the alternative lifestyle (whatever that means) did not surface until he announced that he was gay in a car that was full of my freshman college friends. This statement was followed by an uneasy silence for the rest of the ride. I remember talking when we arrived home. I remember suddenly having to really believe my conviction that being gay was not a bad thing even though I was grossed out. However, I think most of that was just thinking about my brother being a sexual being. The classic line that we both remember was me saying, "But, Jim, I thought you wanted to be a priest!" At the time the irony was lost on me, which is a testament to growing up in a liberal Catholic parish. Also, it felt safer and more comfortable to think of Jim in a celibate role.

I think at the time Jim gave me more credit than I deserved. I believe he thought his "cool" younger sister would be instantly hip to what it means to be gay. I believe Jim's high opinion of me helped me rise to the occasion. When he returned to college, I felt isolated in dealing with my loss . . . not just loss, but anguish. I never felt like I lost Jim since I never had the parental hopes of the stereotypical American dream for Jim. However, I felt pained by the fact that I knew it would be a tough road for him and I knew it would mean changes for me too. I could no longer look the other way when people casually or maliciously made insulting gay comments. I was shocked to register how often this happened. It took years before I was comfortable speaking up and letting people know how I felt about such comments.

When Jim came out to me, I had self-imposed isolation from my family. Now I wish that I had had a good circle of friends I could have shared my angst and concern with. I was desperately trying to fit in and be cool at college, so I didn't take any risks by opening up about my brother. Ironically, one of the friends who was in the car that night, experienced a similar emotional disturbance when two of his brothers came out later that year. Unfortunately, by that time we had gone our separate ways, otherwise we could have given each other much needed support.

Through the years, as I have gained self-confidence, being completely open about Jim has become second nature and a good way to educate people. I think his sexual orientation has helped me explore and become more comfortable with my own sexuality. It has certainly spurred my interest in gender studies. After all, we both live in a culture that is much more accepting if we don't act on our sexual desires.

I have always known that Jim's sexuality does not define him, but is simply a part of a wonderful package. He has always been my oldest sibling and a truly unique person. His being homosexual is the "icing on the cake." By that I mean that Jim's being gay brings a diversity into my life that wouldn't otherwise be there. In turn that experience has helped me understand discrimination and oppression more deeply than I did before. It's made me a better person.

I am grateful that Jim is my brother and my children's uncle. His presence in their lives models the normalness of a person who is gay, or put another way the individuality and goodness of every person. It is reassuring to know that Jim and the rest of our family will help my children understand, cope, and act in positive ways to help stop insensitive and hurtful behavior aimed at people who are homosexual, whether it is themselves or others.

Dan's Story

Dan was the last in the immediate family to know. Though I had tried to maintain a "hands-off" policy regarding Jim's coming out to other family members and let it be his decision, once Dan graduated from high school I remember talking to Jim about telling Dan. I was becoming uncomfortable that Dan was the only one who didn't know and feared he would feel left out of the family circle. There are issues of family trust at stake and I believe it was a mistake to wait so long to tell him.

Dan is Jim's youngest brother—four and a half years younger. Not a great age difference, but enough that they were not really close in spite of the fact that they shared many interests, particularly literature, drama and music. Perhaps because of those shared interests, a rivalry developed between them that exists still today. Dan's account is moving for its honesty and candor.

Jim did not come out of the closet to me directly. My mother told me. She told me at least two years after Jim had informed the rest of the family. I believe I was still in college or maybe I had just gotten sober, as I am a recovering alcoholic. The explanations given for my late enlightenment were: one, I was not mature enough to handle the news; two, Jim feared a violent reaction from me. I understand why Jim was afraid I would react violently. During the height of my drinking career I wanted nothing to do with anyone, I just wanted to be left alone. This came out at family gatherings like Thanksgiving and Christmas, as anger directed at my family. It really was my alcoholism looking for an excuse to get me out of the house and into a bar. Jim caught the bulk of the anger as I perceived him as the "golden child", receiving the most love, adoration, and attention from our parents. For years I took the delayed coming out personally, but today I understand that it had a lot to do with who I was and how I behaved.

Just before I went to college back in 1987, I hung out and drank with a bunch of people. One of them, Dan, was gay. My best drinking buddy's sister was a lesbian. I remember talking to Jim once about Dan. He was involved in theatre and had a similar disposition to Jim's and I thought they would benefit from meeting each other. I remember saying, "even though he is gay, he is a neat guy." Jim's response was something to the effect of, "Oh you already know some gay people and are friends with them?" From that point I just assumed that Jim was gay, and it really didn't change my feelings or thoughts about him. Neither has Jim's coming out affected my feelings and thoughts about gays and lesbians. They are people who have their own likes and dislikes. I have friends that are gay and friends who are not gay. They are all my friends just the same. I understand that I am probably not the norm in this belief.

Jim's coming out has affected me in an indirect way. A parent myself now of four beautiful children, I realize a parent's time to attend to each of his/her children is finite. As a result of Jim's coming out, our parents devote the majority of their lives to advocating for gay rights in the secular and Roman Catholic communities. While for years I separated myself from my family as a result of being a drunk, it has been difficult to regain any relationship. Jim's life is not defined by being gay. He is many other things: a good person, a hard worker, a playwright, a director, a Catholic, a vocalist, a traveler, a brother, an uncle, a son, and much more; as we all are. Our parents' lives seem to be defined by the sole fact that he is gay. It is difficult to find time for my family to spend with my parents to share the things we enjoy and find important in our lives. Most of their evenings and weekends are filled pursuing gay and lesbian rights. This has left me, once again, feeling that what is important to Jim is more important than the other children and grandchildren.

Andy's Story

Andy and Jim are less than a year apart in age. Because of Andy's natural compassion for people in need, people on the margins, I had little doubt he would be accepting and supportive of his brother, but when I asked him to write out his story, he hesitated and confessed to being embarrassed by his initial reaction when Jim came out to him. I believe Andy's story mirrors the struggle of many brothers and sisters—raised in a society hostile to homosexual people—when they learn a sibling is lesbian or gay. It is also a story of conversion.

> When my mom asked me to write about when my brother told me he was gay and my reaction to his revelation, I was reluctant since I am ashamed of the homophobic views that I held at the time. In putting my recollections on paper I hope to own up to my once bigoted views and hopefully leave them further behind.

> I believe it was late summer in 1984 or 1985 when my brother, Jim, told me he was gay. I remember that he was getting ready to go back to college in Ohio and was packing up his car late at night, planning on leaving the next day. Seemingly out of nowhere, Jim asked me what I thought about gays and lesbians. Being more interested in the TV show I was watching, and not catching the huge hint, I said something like: "As long as they leave me alone, I am fine with them." After that, he told me he was gay, and I didn't know what to say. I was silent after that and, as far as I remember, neither of us said anything the rest of the night to each other about it. I think I was mostly embarrassed about the way I answered his question and also a bit confused.

At that time I had not given much thought to homosexuality and the views I had formed regarding homosexuality were informed, or more correctly misinformed, by my friends' homophobic jokes and media stereotypes. I also think that my negative reaction to Jim's inquiry about gays had something to do with the fact that the night before I had been downtown and, while walking by a gay bar, someone made some comment to me like, "nice ass." It upset me more than it should have. I now realize that the anger I felt was partly because of being objectified – a common experience for a woman, but a first for me. I was also upset because I did not want to believe that a gay man would find me attractive. I suppose I felt that it somehow made me less of a man, and I certainly didn't want to be labeled as gay myself. My friends' homophobic views had been rubbing off on me and this incident seemed to further harden my views.

It was difficult to sort out my feelings about Jim's revelation. We did not talk to each other very much. Our interests were quite different, and I think I was a little jealous that my parents seemed to be more interested in Jim's pursuits than mine. I have always admired and respected Jim, even though we have not always seen eye-to-eye. At that time I would not have thought of voicing this fact to him (whether he had come out to me or not). Like many teens, I was very self-centered and other siblings were usually seen as nuisances rather than as friends. It is a shame that I could not have seen past our petty differences and let him know that I respected him and that the fact of his being gay did not change that. I'm sure it would have made the whole experience easier for him.

I remember when growing up, that "fag" and "homo" were probably the worst names that someone could call a male, unless you were one of the very few non-Caucasians in my town. I do not remember hearing anything good about homosexuals. The only gay characters I remember seeing on TV were the gay couple who was occasionally on the *Barney Miller* show. That gay couple was a stereotype: one effeminate person in the woman's submissive role and the other partner in the man's role—neither character was strong—and their sexual orientation was their primary characteristic. While the characters were not portrayed as bad or evil, they were there for comic relief—not to be taken seriously. I understood that the show was a comedy, and that most characters were bound to be caricatures; however, this show was one of the few places where I encountered the subject of homosexuality at all.

During my college years I got involved in a group called Central America Peace Project (CAPP) and got to be good friends with many of the members. As I became more active and learned more, I started making connections between different types of prejudice, authoritarianism and repression. When I went to a non-violence workshop, I had an opportunity to confront some of my prejudices regarding sexual orientation. I think it was here that I first encountered openly gay people (besides Jim). They were people that I admired for their work in promoting peace and social justice, and for their commitment to non-violence. The discussions and experiences that I had at that workshop had a major impact on my views of homosexuality, and from then on I have regarded prejudice against homosexuals the same as any other irrational and hateful view based on fear and ignorance.

I think that I have always known that there was no logical reason that one's sexual orientation was a characteristic that was inherently bad or good, and I knew that prejudice and hatred based on sexual orientation was wrong. I think that's why I felt embarrassed when Jim told me he was gay. I knew I had nothing intelligent to say, and he made me realize that. It just took me a while to lose my brainwashing. Like many irrational ideas and outright lies, if they are stated loud enough and often enough, people are going to believe them – and believe them strongly, since they are impossible to defend in a rational manner.

In the years following the non-violence workshop, I have tried to be somewhat active in supporting gay and lesbian rights. As an activist, I believe that breaking down barriers of prejudice and hatred help all people not just the victims of the prejudice. But I felt a particular need to help organizations fighting prejudice against gays and lesbians, since my brother is a potential target for such prejudice.

Since becoming interested in the law, I have found that one of the biggest myths about gays and lesbians is that civil rights laws and ordinances which include protection for gays and lesbians effectively give them "special rights." The Oregon Citizens Alliance, a group that campaigns against equal rights for lesbian and gay Oregonians, has used this myth as their primary argument in favor of its anti-gay initiatives. Fortunately, the courts have struck down these laws as unconstitutional. In fact, these anti-gay initiatives, if they became laws, would take away rights of lesbian and gay citizens, and would limit their ability to participate in the political process.

I have always found it easier to discuss the political rather than the personal, as is evident by my choice to research gay and lesbian issues rather than talk directly to my brother about what it means for him to be gay. In the more than 18 years since he came out to me, Jim and I have led very different lives: he lives on the East Coast and I live on the West Coast; he lives in a very large cosmopolitan city and I live in a small city; I have a family and Jim has a large, supportive network of friends, but does not have a serious partner. Despite these differences, we have kept in touch through periodic family visits and via email messages and have even had some quite personal, thought provoking discussions. We have also discussed gay and lesbian issues and Jim knows that I support gay rights. However, I don't recall in all these years if I have personally told Jim that I admire, respect and love him, for who he is, including the fact that he is a gay man. I hope he realizes that I do feel this way.

We Can't Tell Grandpa (Grandma), It Would Kill Him (Her)!

Spouses say this to each other. Gay children and their non-gay siblings say it about their grandparents. Parents say it at PFLAG meetings. Where does this stereotype of the uninformed, sheltered, physically weak and emotionally defenseless grandparent come from? In my experience, most grandparents are in touch with the world. They watch TV, go to the movies, read newspapers, magazines and books. Many of them, even in retirement, stay active as volunteers. They are intelligent human beings and they know what goes on in the world. Do they have their blind spots? Of course they do, and they can be just as prejudiced as any one else. But ignorance and prejudice are not an inevitable part of the aging process; they are not given characteristics of being older. In fact, simply by virtue of having lived longer and endured more strife and loss, they may have a better appreciation of what is truly important in life.

Because the survey did not address the feelings of grandparents, I must rely on my own experience. My father, Jim's maternal grandfather, if anything, had mellowed with age. However, he had always been of a conservative, authoritarian mindset, with very definite feelings and opinions on most topics. I was in no hurry to broach this topic with him. He lived in Oregon, thousands of miles away, and had never been especially involved with my life after my marriage. We were not estranged, we simply didn't have much in common and were both caught up in living our own lives. We'd keep in touch with occasional letters and phone calls and perhaps see each other every other year or so. I kept my Dad up-to-date as our kids grew up and left home to go to college and begin to make their own lives. I rarely got into details. However, in the fall of 1992 Oregon had a proposition on the election ballot that would, if passed, prohibit any county or municipality from enacting legislation that would specifically include gay and lesbian people under civil rights protection. That's what it took for me to tell my dad that he had a gay grandson. I simply could not let my dad vote without knowing that his vote could impact, one way or the other, thousands of men and women like his grandson. So early in October of 1992, I wrote dad a long letter telling him Jim is gay. Weeks went by and there was no response, so the weekend before Election Day, I called and asked if he had received my letter and if he had any questions. He said he had received it and that any questions he had he would address to Jim. I said that was fair and I was sure Jim would be happy to talk with him any time. Then, with agitation in his voice, he said, "I just know one thing. They aren't born that way." His tone of voice sent the clear message that "that way" was the wrong way, the bad way. I don't believe he realized the blame implied in his statement. Blaming me for being a bad mother, raising a homosexual son. Blaming Jim for "choosing" to be homosexual. I thought I had prepared myself for a negative response, but I found the anger rushing into my consciousness and out of my mouth. I clenched my teeth and as calmly as I could said, "Dad, you're treading on thin ice here." At that, I heard my stepmother's voice on the phone extension saying, "We still love Jim." That's all I remember of the conversation. I don't know how my dad voted on that proposition. I never asked. We never talked about Jim being gay again. My Dad died in 1994.

Jim's paternal grandparents present a different story altogether. They lived several hundred miles away but that was close enough for them to frequently see the children as they grew up. But that distance still made it easier to keep this "news" about Jim from them. Initially Jim wasn't ready to tell them, and as time went by it became easier to just let it slide. What was to be gained by telling them, we rationalized. It wouldn't be fair. We'd only be giving them something more to worry about. And that strategy worked pretty well until Casey and I got involved with Catholic Gay & Lesbian Family Ministry in our diocese. It became difficult to explain why we were so busy with "volunteer" work without explaining what the work was about. Finally keeping the secret became more difficult than dealing with the truth and we talked to Jim about telling them. By that time, I guess Jim had enough confidence in us that he requested that we do the honors.

Before we told Casey's parents, the kids and I would have occasional debates about whether they already knew or not. We know how parents can use denial as an effective tool to delay dealing with a situation they just want to disappear, and we suspected that grandparents have the same facility for denial. Let me illustrate. Jim's senior college thesis project took the form of a play that he wrote and directed. The play, entitled *David and Jonathan*[3] was about a college student coming out to his parents. Jim patterned his fictional family on his own, and we had a few uncomfortable—yet humorous—moments as we sat in the audience, recognizing what was fact in the fictional play—all the time hoping the rest of the audience believed it was all fiction. Jim's grandparents joined us for one of the performances and we thought this might be a relatively painless way to bring up the subject and tell them about Jim. Actually, we figured we wouldn't have to tell them, that they would know based on the play they had just seen. I remember talking with our daughter after the play, speculating whether they had figured it out or not. Her sardonic response was, "I don't *think* so, Mom. I just talked to Grandma and she asked me if the assistant director is Jim's girlfriend." (If she only knew! The assistant director, a good friend of Jim's, was a lesbian woman.) In the end, we lost our nerve and remained silent.

When we finally did tell them, it was no big deal. Grandma had a few questions then, and on occasion has more questions, often sparked by something she's heard or read. Grandpa was his usual silent, stoic self, though I suspect that some of Grandma's questions were really his.

A few years after we told them, we had a weeklong family reunion. Casey's mom and dad and his brother were there, along with our children, including spouses or any "special friends." Jim brought Ed, a good friend whom he had known for several years. At the end of the week, as goodbye hugs and kisses traveled through the group, I witnessed a small scene that will remain in my heart forever. Grandpa, in his direct way, simply shook Ed's hand and said, "Ed, you take good care of Jimmy, now."

If we had not told Casey's parents, I would not have that memory. Jim would not know the fullness of their love and affirmation of him, and perhaps most importantly, Grandma and Grandpa would not have had the opportunity to know and love Jim so fully.

Conclusion

"Fortunate families"—moms and dads, brothers and sisters, grandparents, aunts and uncles and cousins—don't exist in silence and secrecy. They share the truth of who they are and, like Jim's siblings and grandparents, each family member travels his or her own unique path to understanding. The love of Dan, Linda and Andy for their brother, Jim, who is gay, will model for their own children a love and understanding that will change the world. For our part, Casey and I hope that what we do—not *for* Jim, but *because* of Jim—will help make a difference. In the back of our minds there is always the possibility that what we do now might make life a little easier for a grandchild who discovers she is lesbian or he is gay. The love, support and understanding of all our children is just one more thing that makes ours a fortunate family.

Notes

1   Dew, Robb Forman, (1994) *The Family Heart: A Memoir of When Our Son Came Out*. New York: Addison-Wesley Publishing Company.

2   Dew, p. 222.

3   The title, *David & Jonathan*, is an allusion to the Hebrew Scripture story of David's love for Jonathan, the son of Saul.

6

Phil's Story:
"My son is no joking matter"

Phil and Ann were married over 42 years ago—outside the communion rail, because Phil was not Catholic. After a few years, Phil converted to Catholicism. They have five grown children and three grandchildren. Ann has worked as a secretary for her diocese and parish. Phil, now retired, worked for a large man-ufacturing company. He continues to be involved with the church men's group. Here is his story.

> It was the early 1980's when our son, Tim, came to me and said he had something to tell me. Then, nervously, he told me that he is gay. Initially, I was very upset with him. Even though I'd had my suspicions about it for a while, I'd never said anything even to my wife, Ann. I was upset because he was our first born son and I was not happy that his life had taken this turn—that he would never marry or have children. In talking it over with my wife, who really pursued more information about homosexuality after Tim told her, I finally realized it was not as bad as I first thought. I have come to accept the fact and it doesn't bother me any more. He is our son and we love him.

As time went on, I never mentioned Tim's being gay to any of my friends at work or socially. Then one day when I was picking up some parts for a job at the maintenance department of the manufacturing company where I worked, there were two guys there telling jokes about homosexuals and using the word "faggot" repeatedly. I knew one of the men but not the other. It upset me hearing this kind of talk about gay people now that I knew I had a gay son. After hearing "faggot" about four times, I became very angry and told them I didn't appreciate the stupid joke because I have a gay son and didn't like the word they were using. Then I left the area. The next day the man I didn't know came up to me and was very apologetic. He said he didn't really feel that way, but just was going along with it. He said he was embarrassed and sorry he had acted like that. The man I knew never mentioned anything about the incident to me, as if it never happened.

Another time, at a party sponsored by a Catholic men's group, a similar thing happened and I felt that I had to say something. After hearing joking about gay people at the dinner table, I told the men that my son—who most of them knew—is gay. Everyone became quiet and never spoke that way again around Ann or me. They now accept Tim for who he is and treat him no differently than our other children.

When Tim met his first partner and they got an apartment together, he was anxious for us to meet this man. At first, I didn't want to—I was still uncomfortable with him actually having a gay partner. Then one day, they invited us to their place for dinner. Ann wanted to go and I said, "Okay, I'll go too." Well, I was pleasantly surprised. The meal was delicious, their place was really nice, and I got along very well with Tim's partner. I found we had similar interests and he had a great sense of humor.

Now we are very open about our son's homosexuality and never hesitate to talk about it if the occasion arises. Our friends and family are also very accepting of Tim—his being gay is just a fact of life now. Sometimes, people who have learned that someone close to them is gay contact us, just to have someone to talk to about it. Friends and family members have confided in us, and we have tried to help them to accept their gay loved one. Ann and I did not have anyone to turn to when we found out Tim was gay. We understand now how much that means to other parents.

7

Church Teaching, Pastoral Care & My Son
By Casey Lopata

In this chapter, Casey addresses church teaching in relation to homosexuality and the questions that parents may have when a son or daughter comes out to them. Casey offers a distinctive father's perspective.

My Son, Gay and Catholic

Like a kid, I wandered through the exhibit booths of the first Call To Action conference (CTA), called by the U.S. Bishops and held in Detroit in 1976, eagerly sampling whatever Vatican II presents I could get my hands on! Collecting brochures, as though they were free samples at a candy store, I only glanced at each long enough to confirm its affirmation of my beliefs before reaching for the next. Then, like unexpectedly coming upon a green bean among the candy samples, I pulled up short as I read the favorable messages about homosexuality posted on the "Dignity" booth. Collecting myself, I made a discreet detour, quickly dismissed this aberration and continued merrily on my sampling trip.

That's my earliest remembrance of any conscious thought about homosexuality. I was 35 years old and totally ignorant about homosexuality. My vague understanding of church teaching was: Homosexuality was wrong. Period! Like osmosis, the deafening silence surrounding homosexuality had seeped into my consciousness and left me with the notion that homosexuality was something to avoid; it was bad, and totally incongruous in such a church-related setting.

Seven years later, I was still ignorant. Like my unthinking collecting of brochures at Call To Action, I was still unthinkingly collecting messages from society and church that coalesced into a muddled belief that homosexuality was not only a sin, but the worst sin of all. So when Jim said, "Dad, I'm gay," his words were literally unthinkable for me. Jim told me as he drove me to the airport for a business trip. My internal reaction was, how could this be? I mumbled something about, "Are you sure?" (Yes), and, "Is this something you can change?" (No). Then our brief conversation ended as Jim dropped me off at the terminal.

Rationality! That's what I needed to bring to my irrational beliefs, and to my unacknowledged feelings! I was forced to wrestle with Jim's revelation on the trip, and for weeks after. My strong social justice beliefs nurtured by the church and my internal understanding that "homosexuality was bad, period!" came together to form the one question I needed to answer: Can Jim be gay AND a faithful Catholic?

That became THE question for me. While Mary Ellen rode the emotional guilt/doubt/grief roller coaster typified in many stories about parents' journeys, I logically stepped my way through a theological minefield. That's what you do when Vatican documents are light reading for you, and you nearly fall off the thinker side of those thinker versus feeler scales. And that's what you do when you have no related experience to draw on, for I didn't know any homosexual people. (Of course, I did; I just didn't know that they were gay).

Systematically analyzing whether Jim could be gay *and* Catholic, my first logical step was to try to think back to the day when I decided whether I was going to be homosexual or heterosexual. I couldn't remember such a day because I never made that decision, nor did Jim nor anyone else I've talked with about this. I discovered that church documents talk of the given, fixed nature of sexual orientation. For example, the U.S. Bishops refer to "those persons for whom homosexuality is a permanent, seemingly irreversible sexual orientation,"[1] and their Committee on Marriage and Family says, "Generally, homosexual orientation is experienced as a given, not as something freely chosen."[2]

Learning that Jim didn't choose his homosexuality was a giant first step for me. What should have been obvious, wasn't. As I've heard gay people say: "Why would I choose to be gay when I know gay people lose jobs and homes simply because they're gay, they are publicly vilified, and some even die simply because they're gay?" For example, in Michigan Jim could be a model employee and a model tenant, yet be fired or evicted just because he is gay. As of June 2003, only 14 states have laws barring discrimination based on sexual orientation.[3]

The notion that homosexuality is a choice was perhaps the predominant myth I had assimilated from society. That was a powerful learned belief. So my journey of reconciling Jim's homosexuality with my faith was one, not only of education, but also of a conversion of heart.

Though not a choice, still I wondered, "Why does Jim have this orientation?" Scientists didn't start studying this concept until the mid-1800s, and the Catholic Church didn't officially acknowledge sexual orientation until 1975. I learned from the American Psychological Association (APA) that "many scientists share the view that sexual orientation is shaped for most people at an *early age* through *complex* interactions of biological, psychological and social factors." . . . and that "scientific evidence does not show that conversion therapy works and that it can do more harm than good."[4] In July 1998, the APA stated explicitly:

> [H]uman beings cannot choose to be either gay or straight. Sexual orientation emerges for most people in early adolescence without any prior sexual experience. Although we can choose whether or not to act on our feelings, psychologists do not consider sexual orientation to be a conscious choice that can be voluntarily changed.[5]

And church teaching says:

> Sexuality . . . is a fundamental dimension of every human being. It is reflected physiologically, psychologically, and relationally in a

person's gender identity as well as in one's primary sexual orientation and behavior. For some young men and women, that means a discovery that one is homosexual . . .[6]

The Church also teaches that sexuality is a gift, and "sexual identity helps to define the unique persons we are, and one component of our sexual identity is sexual orientation."[7]

I came to understand sexual orientation is not our choice. How to *act* on our orientation—that's our choice. I also learned Jim is not an anomaly. The Catechism says: "The number of men and women who have deep-seated homosexual tendencies is not negligible."[8] Using a conservative 3% (based on estimates of 1-10% of the population being homosexual), I calculated that our diocese could have over 10,000 gay or lesbian Catholics! There was some comfort in knowing that those 10,000 all had parents, some of whom undoubtedly lived in our parish. We knew we weren't alone in our struggle, but there was no way of connecting with those other parents, no way we could support one another. So the journey remained a lonely, isolated one.

I then asked: What about sin? Is homosexuality a sin? To my surprise, the Vatican unequivocally states: "The particular inclination of a homosexual person is not a sin."[9] Of course! A homosexual orientation can't be a sin if it's not a choice. As *Always Our Children* says: "Generally, homosexual orientation is experienced as a given, not as something freely chosen. By itself, therefore, a homosexual orientation cannot be considered sinful, for morality presumes the freedom to choose."[10] This made even more sense to me when I came to understand that being homosexual is something Jim IS, not something Jim does, just like being heterosexual is something I AM, not something I do.

Finally I realized what this means. When I was 15, those romantic feelings I had for Annette Funicello were not a sin! (For you youngsters, Annette was the young, pretty female star of the Mickey Mouse Club TV show. Today it might be Jennifer Aniston, Cameron Diaz, Britney Spears or some other young female entertainment figure.) My feelings weren't about having sex with Annette, but feelings of wanting to be with her, wanting to get to know her. Those romantic feelings of "falling in love" were OK. It was clear that if Jim had seen reruns of the Mickey Mouse Club when he was 15, and if Jim had those same romantic feelings for one of the male stars, that was okay. The Catholic Church says Jim's romantic feelings for someone of the same sex are not a sin. That's what having a sexual orientation is all about. People with a homosexual orientation are simply people who fall in love with another person of the same sex.[11]

But what about what these feelings might lead to? What about homogenital acts? This must be where I'll learn that homosexual acts are so bad you can't even talk about them! As I expected, the Vatican says: "It is only in the marital relationship that the use of the sexual faculty can be morally good."[12] And the U.S. Bishops say: "Homosexual activity . . . as distinguished from homosexual orientation, is morally wrong." But, they continue: "Like heterosexual persons, homosexuals are called to give witness to chastity, avoiding, with God's grace, behavior which is wrong for them, just as non-marital sexual relations are wrong for heterosexuals."[13] What hit me—probably because I'm heterosexual—is the part that says: *"just as* non-marital sexual relations are wrong for heterosexuals."

This tells me if Jim has sexual relations outside of marriage, he violates church-established moral norms; just like my heterosexual children, if they have sexual relations outside of marriage, or if they use artificial birth control, or if they masturbate. The Catholic Church uses words like "intrinsically and gravely disordered" to describe all of these acts. Yet I knew if my daughter, Linda, concerned about artificial birth control, and Jim, concerned about homogenital activity, sought pastoral counseling from the same priests or pastoral ministers, Jim would hear words like "intrinsically and gravely disordered" far more frequently than Linda.

With that pastoral inconsistency simmering in my subconscious, I progressed to my next question: Since church law restricts marriage to a man and woman, does this mean homogenital behavior is *always* a sin? The Vatican says: "In fact, circumstances may exist, or may have existed in the past, which would reduce or remove the culpability of the individual [engaged in homosexual activity] . . . in a given instance."[14] So Church teaching says homogenital acts are not necessarily always a sin. Of course! Years before I had learned from the Baltimore Catechism that three things are necessary for mortal sin: 1) the thought, desire, word, action or omission must be seriously wrong, 2) the person must know it's seriously wrong, and 3) the person must fully consent to it. What's important to remember is that only God knows how knowledgeable and how free each of us really is. The new Catholic Catechism says it this way: "Imputability and responsibility for an action can be diminished or even nullified by ignorance, inadvertence, duress, fear, habit, inordinate attachments, and other psychological or social factors."[15] Practically, this means that no one knows if persons who fall short of the moral norms of the church—whether it be a married couple using artificial contraception or a same-sex couple in a sexual relationship—are committing a sin. Only God can judge the subjective factors of the individuals involved. That's why, though the church has a long list of people believed to be in heaven—we call them "saints"—there is no corresponding list of people who are definitively in hell, no matter how horrific their outward behavior may have been.

I also learned that the church recommends a pastoral approach. For example, one theologian who authored a Vatican document about sexuality, in a newspaper interview discussing the document, said: "When one is dealing with people who are so predominately homosexual that they will be in serious personal and perhaps social trouble unless they attain a steady partnership within their homosexual lives, one can recommend them to seek such a partnership and one accepts this relationship as the best they can do in their present situation."[16] This is based on the moral principle that no one is obliged to do what is impossible for him or her to do. In its guidelines for confessors concerning some aspects of the morality of conjugal life, the Pontifical Council for the Family offers the following application of this principle: "the confessor is to avoid demonstrating lack of trust in the grace of God or in the dispositions of the penitent by exacting humanly impossible absolute guarantees of an irreproachable future conduct."[17]

Concerning the Bible, I learned that Catholic teaching says six biblical texts clearly say homosexual behavior is immoral.[18] The six texts are: Genesis 19: 1-11 (the story of Sodom); Leviticus 18:22 and 20:13 (man lying with a man as with a woman); I Corinthians 6:9 ("sodomites" and others not inheriting the kingdom of God); Romans 1:18-32 (giving up natural intercourse for unnatural); I Timothy 1:10 ("sodomites" and others as lawless and disobedient). But I also read Victor Paul Furnish, Daniel Helminiak, Robin Scroggs and many other biblical scholars who, using Catholic methods of scripture interpretation, convincingly argue the Bible is not really so clear on this. These various authors point out, for example:

1. There are only six passages generally used to condemn homosexuality.

2. The primary concern of these passages is something other than homogenital activity.

3. There are translation issues suggested by the fact that 1946 was the first time the word "homosexual" appeared in an English translation.

4. The biblical writers had no concept of our modern psychological understanding of homosexual orientation.

5. The prophets, the gospels and Jesus say nothing about homosexuality in the bible.

The lack of clarity is magnified when one considers these passages in the light of the Bible's primary message to love God and love your neighbor as yourself, and by gospel themes such as faithfulness, justice, mutuality, alienation, forgiveness and compassion. I concluded that no matter how we interpret these passages, we should use them very carefully or not at all, just as we carefully use or ignore passages that say all who curse their mother or father should be put to death (Leviticus 20:9); passages that tell women to keep silent in church (1 Timothy 2:11-14); or passages that clearly support slavery (Ephesians 6: 5-9, 1 Timothy 6: 1-2, Titus 2: 9-10 and 1 Peter 2: 18-19).

So at this point in my journey—and it actually was a meandering many-year process, not the series of logical steps I've presented here—I'd learned that it's not a sin for Jim to have a homosexual orientation, and that Jim can be gay and a faithful Catholic, just like any other faithful Catholic who struggles with objective moral norms established by the church. In a 1976 document, the U.S. Bishops summed up what our approach should be so well that they repeated it in their 1991 document: "Homosexual [persons], like everyone else, should not suffer from prejudice against their basic human rights. They have a right to respect, friendship, and justice. They should have an active role in the Christian community."[19]

Through this process, I also learned that a thinker like me has feelings too! Since my son is gay, I'm personally affected by this teaching, and I would like some of it to change. And that's okay, because none of this teaching is infallible. By definition, it could change, and with my knowledge and experience, I have something to add to the discussion.[20] In fact, teaching on sexuality has changed. For example, it wasn't until 1951 that the use of a woman's sterile period for the deliberate purpose of avoiding conception was explicitly approved.[21] And it was Vatican II that first recognized the mutual love of the spouses as co-equal to the procreation and education of children as primary purposes of marriage—not procreation only.[22]

But the question remains, will teaching on homosexuality change? Change springs from unresolved tensions, and there are several unresolved tensions around Catholic teaching and homosexuality. In addition to the tension of biblical interpretation described earlier, here are four others that I believe could be catalysts for change in Catholic teaching depending on how they are resolved.

First tension: The Catholic Church says it's okay to be homosexual as long as one lives celibately, yet the church also teaches that celibacy is a gift. Technically celibacy is the foregoing of marriage for religious reasons, but current usage has broadened that definition to mean sexual abstinence. Practically, the question is: Are all gay people gifted with the ability to live a life of sexual abstinence? Catholic parents of gay sons and lesbian daughters feel this tension when asked about their understanding of church teaching. In the survey, 68% agreed with this statement: "A homosexual orientation is not sinful, but any homosexual genital activity is sinful." Yet only 41% agreed with the statement: "A life of total sexual abstinence is required of all homosexual persons."

Second tension: Catholic teaching considers homosexual orientation to be a sexual *deviation*, a "disorder." The church also teaches there can be no conflict between faith and reason, yet the American Psychiatric Association, the American Psychological Association, and virtually all of the scientific community consider homosexual orientation to be a natural sexual *variation*. This example isn't completely appropriate because it compares the church's philosophical definition with the scientific community's psychological definition; however, the confusion itself is one reason for the tension.

Third tension: The voices of gay and lesbian Catholics are not evident in most church documents, effectively denying their experience in the life of the church. They are surely not reflected in statements like these from various Catholic documents:

1. Although the particular inclination of the homosexual person is not a sin, it is a more or less strong tendency ordered toward an intrinsic moral evil; and thus the inclination itself must be seen as an objective moral evil.[23]

2. [W]hen they engage in homosexual activity they confirm within themselves a disordered sexual inclination which is essentially self-indulgent.[24]

3. Even when the practice of homosexuality may seriously threaten the lives and well being of a large number of people, its advocates remain undeterred and refuse to consider the magnitude of the risks involved.[25]

4. But the proper reaction to crimes committed against homosexual persons should not be to claim that the homosexual condition is not disordered. When such a claim is made and when homosexual activity is consequently condoned, or when civil legislation is introduced to protect behavior to which no one has any conceivable right, neither the Church nor society at large should be surprised when other distorted notions and practices gain ground, and irrational and violent reactions increase.[26]

5. There are areas in which it is not unjust discrimination to take sexual orientation into account, for example, in the placement of children for adoption or foster care, in employment of teachers or athletic coaches, and in military recruitment.[27]

6. An individual's sexual orientation is generally not known to others unless he publicly identifies himself as having this orientation or unless some overt behavior manifests it. As a rule, the majority of homosexually oriented persons who seek to lead chaste lives do not publicize their orientation. Hence, the problem of discrimination on terms of employment, housing, etc. does not usually arise.[28]

The impact of centuries of these kinds of implicit and explicit negative messages about sexuality in general and homosexuality in particular has produced deep-seated attitudes. Perhaps this is why, in the survey, only 14% of parents believed the church teaches that: "Our sexuality, whether homosexual or heterosexual, is a gift from God." This, despite official Catholic teaching that says, "A deep respect for the total person leads the Church to hold and teach that sexuality is a gift from God."[29]

In contrast, the writers of *Always Our Children* clearly listened to and used what they heard from parents when formulating statements like these:

1. You may still insist: "You are always my child; nothing can ever change that. You are also a child of God, gifted and called for a purpose in God's design."[30]

2. God loves every person as a unique individual. Sexual identity helps to define the unique persons we are, and one component of our sexual identity is sexual orientation.[31]

3. God does not love anyone less simply because he or she is homosexual.[32]

4. The teachings of the Church make it clear that the fundamental rights of homosexual persons must be defended and that all of us must strive to eliminate any forms of injustice, oppression, or violence against them. It is not sufficient only to avoid unjust discrimination. Homosexual persons must be treated with respect, compassion and sensitivity.[33]

5. Nothing in the Bible or in Catholic teaching can be used to justify prejudicial or discriminatory attitudes or behaviors.[34]

6. To our homosexual brothers and sisters we offer a concluding word . . . Though at times you may feel discouraged, hurt, or angry, do not walk away from your families, from the Christian community, from all those who love you. In you, God's love is revealed. You are always our children.[35]

Catholic teaching was formulated without the participation of openly gay and lesbian people, and the teaching doesn't take into account the lived experience of faithful, gay and lesbian Catholics: real people, made in the image and likeness of God, who, like all of us, struggle to do what God calls us to do. When will the voices of gay and lesbian people be reflected in a church document? We can only hope that the words of John Paul II, discussing "solidarity," will be applied to this void. John Paul II said: "[T]he structure must not only allow the emergence of the opposition, give it the opportunity to express itself, but also must make it possible for the opposition to function for the good of the community."[36]

Finally, the *fourth tension*: The church teaches that same-sex marriage is unacceptable. Yet it also teaches: "Whether it develops between persons of the same or opposite sex, friendship represents a great good for all. It leads to spiritual communion."[37] There is a lot of gray area to be explored between these two poles, starting with the teaching: "Friendship, which is a way of loving . . . is essential to healthy human development. It is one of the richest possible human experiences."[38]

These tensions are not just the work of some "dissident" theologians. Some bishops are also questioning church teaching. For example, Bishop Thomas Gumbleton of Detroit, when asked about homosexual orientation as an "objective disorder," said, "I don't feel I have to accept that."[39] Some might argue that Bishop Gumbleton lacks objectivity because he has a gay brother, but he's not alone among bishops in having a gay or lesbian loved one, and he's not alone in his concerns. The U.S. Bishops, in their 1991 document, *Human Sexuality*, relegated the Vatican reference to a homosexual orientation as a "disorder" to a footnote because, as San Francisco Archbishop John Quinn explained, in the text it might be misinterpreted to mean that "homosexual people are evil."[40]

In light of these tensions and cognizant of previous changes in church teaching on sexuality, I believe Rochester Bishop Matthew Clark took a prudent, as well as prophetic, position in response to an interviewer's question about homosexuality. He said: "We need to learn more about this reality. I think the church's present disposition is based on a certain body of facts and experience, and that's to be honored and I intend to honor it. But we need to continue learning from new facts and new experiences and I don't know with enormous clarity what tomorrow's church might say about the issue we're talking about today."[41]

Change in church teaching is possible, but the official church tends to move very, very slowly. However, I need guidance today. That brings me to Catholic teaching on the primacy of conscience. Pope John Paul II puts it this way in *Crossing the Threshold of Hope*: "If man (sic) is admonished by his own conscience—even if an erroneous conscience, but one whose voice appears to him as unquestionable—he must always listen to it. What is not permissible is that he culpably indulge in error without trying to reach the truth."[42] The Catechism puts it concisely: "A human being must *always* [my emphasis] obey the certain judgment of his [or her] conscience. If he [or she] were deliberately to act against it, he [or she] would condemn him [or her] self."[43] That's quite clear, but does it mean we can do anything we want? Of course not! Doing what we want and doing what our conscience dictates are not necessarily the same thing. (Often, perhaps most of the time, our conscience urges us to do what we really don't want to do, e.g. be more loving, thoughtful, generous, less selfish, prideful, greedy, etc.) I recall theologian Charles Curran articulating this tension that we all face: "We *must* obey our conscience, but our conscience might be wrong."

Conscience formation leads to the concept of moral discernment in the Catholic moral tradition.[44] The church suggests looking at experience—our own, and the wisdom of the community especially those whose wisdom and virtue we respect; reason—including the sciences; scripture—using Catholic interpretation principles, not a fundamentalist reading; and tradition, i.e. church teaching. All four areas are important to consider before coming to a responsible decision. Why all four? Because each has been wrong. Consider centuries of societal and church acceptance of the institution of slavery. Consider that it wasn't until the mid-19th century that scientists first explored homosexuality as something a person *was* (orientation), rather than something a person *did*. Consider the biblical acceptance of slavery;[45] for example, 1 Corinthians 7:20-24, Ephesians 6:5-9, Titus 2:9-10, 1 Peter 2:18-19. Consider ecclesial condemnation of the view that the earth moved around the sun.

What if, after we've gone through this discernment process, church teaching and our conscience do not agree? Many Catholics have struggled with this dilemma over the questions of artificial birth control and divorce and remarriage. I learned that Church teaching itself says we should start with the presumption that church teaching is right, including teaching on personal sin, on the primacy of conscience, and on not being expected to do the impossible. Starting with that presumption, one then needs to recognize that all church teaching is not equally authoritative. An encyclical, for example, carries more weight than a letter from a Vatican congregation. Then we take the relative authority of church teachings and weigh them against what we've learned in the other three areas, and ultimately ask: Is our response life serving? Can our response bear public scrutiny? Are we responding to the God revealed in Jesus Christ?[46]

How do we apply this to questions about homosexuality? Perhaps the English and Welsh Bishops said it best:

> Pastoral care does not consist simply in the rigid and automatic application of objective moral norms. It considers the individual in his (or her) actual situation, with all his (or her) strengths and weaknesses. The decision of conscience, determining what should be done and what avoided, can only be made after prudent consideration of the real situation as well as the moral norm . . . pastoral counseling . . . cannot ignore the objective morality of homosexual genital acts, but it is important to interpret them, to under-

stand the pattern of life in which they take place, to appreciate the personal meaning which these acts have for different people . . .[47]

Bishop Thomas Gumbleton demonstrates how to balance church teaching and conscience. When asked what he would teach, Bishop Gumbleton said:

> I will say what the church teaches—that to be actively homosexual is wrong. But every one of us has to come to terms with church teaching and apply it to our own lives in light of our own conscience with the guidance of the church. I don't make judgments about a gay person's conscience any more than about the military man at a SAC air base or on a Trident submarine who would fire a nuclear weapon if ordered to. I think in some ways the church teaching on that is clearer than on homosexuality. Any act of war that would destroy an entire city indiscriminately is an abomination. That is what nuclear weapons are all about. Anybody who has the intention of using such weapons is, in my judgment, in a situation that is drastically evil. And yet I cannot judge another person's conscience. If that person comes to communion, I cannot refuse.[48]

So, after considering church teaching on homosexuality, personal sin, conscience, and discernment, intellectually I found Jim can certainly be gay and Catholic. But this discovery was still in my thinker's world of theology and homosexuality. . . until I heard Bishop Kenneth Untener. Speaking to a largely gay and lesbian audience, he said: "When we die, and as a moral theologian I don't say this lightly, the *only* [my emphasis] thing that will matter is how we treated each other."[49] That's when I realized the final step of my journey was getting to know and love many faithful Catholic gay people, like Sheila, David, Kristin, Bill, Mary Lou, Paul, Lynn, Pat, Jan, Kathy, John and so many others. One mother we know expressed my goal clearly and concisely. About her son, she said: "I don't want to love him despite his homosexuality. I want to embrace him as a homosexual person." Her son, and our son Jim, and the lesbian and gay people named above are concerned citizens, dependable employees, good neighbors, loving family members and caring volunteers. They are people who love God and love their neighbors as themselves. If how we treat each other is what matters most, these gay Catholics will be judged generously. That's how I really know Jim can be gay and Catholic.

Andrew Sullivan says: "Homosexuality—when you actually look at it in people whom you need and love—is a very different issue from when it's some abstract mode of being or some closeted, repressed mode of being, which is equally abstract."[50] As a "head" person, I tend to get so theological I risk forgetting that we're not talking about abstract issues here, but about real people—sons, daughters, aunts, uncles, mothers, fathers, friends. I know of no better reminder of this than the words of the late Westminster Cardinal George Basil Hume:

> Love between two persons, whether of the same sex or of a different sex, is to be treasured and respected. "Jesus loved Martha and her sister and Lazarus," we read (John 11:5). When two persons love, they experience in a limited manner in this world what will be their unending delight when one with God in the next. To love another is in fact to reach out to God, who shares his lovableness with the one we love. To be loved is to receive a sign or share of God's unconditional love. To love another, whether of the same sex or of a different sex, is to have entered the area of the richest human experience.[51]

Notes

1   National Conference of Catholic Bishops (NCCB), *Human Sexuality: A Catholic Perspective for Education and Lifelong Learning*, U.S. Catholic Conference, 1991.

2   National Conference of Catholic Bishops (NCCB), Committee on Marriage and Family, *Always Our Children (AOC.)*, 3rd printing, U.S. Catholic Conference (USCC), Washington, DC, revised June 1998, p. 6.

3   California, Connecticut, Hawaii, Maryland, Massachusetts, Minnesota, Nevada, New Hampshire, New Jersey, New Mexico, New York, Rhode Island, Vermont and Wisconsin, and the District of Columbia.

4   American Psychological Association (APA), *Answers to Your Questions About Sexual Orientation and Homosexuality*, APA, Washington, DC, 1993.

5   American Psychological Association (APA), *Answers to Your Questions About Sexual Orientation and Homosexuality*, APA, Washington, DC, 1998.

6   NCCB, *Human Sexuality*, p. 54.

7   NCCB, *AOC.* p.7.

8   *Catechism of the Catholic Church*, U. S. Catholic Conference, 1994, #2358.

9   Congregation for the Doctrine of the Faith (CDF), *Letter to the Bishops of the Catholic Church on the Pastoral Care of Homosexual Persons (PCHP)*, 1986, # 3.

10   NCCB, *AOC*, p. 6.

11   This analogy was borrowed from Brian McNaught, "Reflections of a Gay Catholic," in *Homosexuality and the Catholic Church*, ed. Jeannine Gramick, Thomas More Press, Chicago, IL, 1983, p. 31-32.

12 CDF, *PCHP*, # 7.

13 NCCB, *To Live in Christ Jesus: A Pastoral Reflection on the Moral Life (ICJ)*, USCC. 1976, # 52.

14 CDF, *PCHP*, # 11.

15 *Catechism of the Catholic Church*, U.S. Catholic Conference, 1994, # 1735.

16 Visser, Jan, quoted by Sean O'Riordan, C.Ss.R., in "The 'Declaration on Certain Questions Concerning Sexual Ethics': A Discussion," James McManus, C.Ss.R., Sean O'Riordan, CSs.R., and Henry Stratton, *The Clergy Review*, London, June 1976, v. 61, no. 6, p. 233.

17 Pontifical Council for the Family (PCF), "Vade Mecum for Confessors Concerning some Aspects of the Morality of Conjugal Life," *Origins*, March 13, 1997.

18 CDF, *PCHP*, #5-6.

19 NCCB, *ICJ*, # 52 and *Human Sexuality*, p. 55.

20 Canon # 212.3. "In accord with the knowledge, competence and the preeminence which they possess, they [the Christian faithful] have the right and even at times the duty to manifest to the sacred pastors their opinion on matters which pertain to the good of the Church, and they have a right to make their opinion known to the other Christian faithful, with due regard for the integrity of faith and morals and reverence toward their pastors, and with consideration for the common good and the dignity of persons."

21 Pius XII, Address to Midwives, 1951.

22 *Constitution on the Church in the Modern World (Gaudium et Spes)* n. 50: "But marriage is not merely for the procreation of children; its nature as an indissoluble compact between two people and the good of the children demand that the mutual love of the partners be properly shown, that it should grow and mature." Vatican II, December 1965.

23 CDF, *PCHP*, # 3.

24 Ibid, # 7.

25 Ibid. # 9.

26 Ibid. #10.

27 Congregation for the Doctrine of the Faith (CDF), *Responding to Legislative Proposals on Discrimination Against Homosexuals (LEG,)* 1992, # 11.

28 Ibid, # 14.

29 NCCB, *AOC*, p. 7.

30 Ibid, p. 4.

31 Ibid, p. 7.

32 Ibid.

33 Ibid, p. 9.

34 Ibid, p. 10

35 Ibid, p. 13.

36 *Karol Wotyla (Pope John Paul II): An Anthology*, edited by Alfred Bloch and George T. Czuczka (NY: Crossroad, 1981), p. 49. John Paul II explains solidarity as "a natural consequence of the fact that a human being exists and acts together with others. Solidarity is also the foundation of a community in which the common good conditions and liberates participation, and participation serves the common good," p. 47.

37 *Catechism of the Catholic Church*, # 2347.

38 NCCB, *AOC*, p. 9.

39 Tom Roberts, "He's Not Disordered, He's My Brother," *National Catholic Reporter*, Nov. 4, 1994, p. 6.

40 Robert Nugent and Jeannine Gramick, *Building Bridges: Gay & Lesbian Reality and the Catholic Church*, 23rd Publications: Mystic, CT, 1992, p. 141.

41 "Clark Plans Mass for Homosexuals," Rochester, NY, *Democrat & Chronicle*, Feb. 19, 1997, p. 5A.

42 John Paul II, *Crossing the Threshold of Hope*, (NY: Alfred A. Knopf, 1994), p. 191.

43 *Catechism of the Catholic Church*, # 1790.

44 NCCB, *Human Sexuality*, see pp. 22-27 for a more complete discussion of Catholic moral discernment.

45 *The Holy Bible, New Revised Standard Version*. New York: Oxford University Press, 1977.

    1 Corinthians 7:20-24: "Let each of you remain in the condition in which you were called. Were you a slave when called? Do not be concerned about it. Even if you can gain your freedom, make use of your present condition now more than ever. For whoever was called in the Lord as a slave is a freed person belonging to the Lord, just as whoever was free when called is a slave of Christ. You were bought with a price; do not become slaves of human masters. In whatever condition you were called, brothers and sisters, there remain with God."

    Ephesians 6:5-9: "Slaves, obey your earthly masters with fear and trembling, in singleness of heart, as you obey Christ; not only while being watched, and in order to please them, but as slaves of Christ, doing the will of God from the heart. Render service with enthusiasm, as to the Lord and not to men and women, knowing that whatever good we do, we will receive the same again from the Lord, whether we are slaves or free. And masters, do the same to them. Stop threatening them, for you know that both of you have the same Master in heaven, and with him there is no partiality."

    Titus 2:9-10: "Tell slaves to be submissive to their masters and to give satisfaction in every respect; they are not to talk back, not to pilfer, but to show complete and perfect fidelity, so that in everything they may be an ornament to the doctrine of God our Savior."

    1 Peter 2:18-19: "slaves, accept the authority of your masters with all deference, not only those who are kind and gentle but also those who are harsh. For it is a credit to you if, being aware of God, you endure pain while suffering unjustly."

46 Fr. Robert J. Kennedy, presentation on moral decision making, as part of *Homosexuality: A Christian Perspective*, at Holy Name Church in Greece, NY, April 23, 1994.

47 Catholic Bishops of England and Wales, Catholic Social Welfare Commission, *An Introduction to the Pastoral Care of Homosexual People: Pastoral Guidelines for Priests*, 1979.

48 Tom Roberts, p. 6.

49 Bishop Kenneth Untener, "Hallmarks of the Church," (Address at New Ways Ministry Symposium, March 28, 1992) in *Voices of Hope*, Eds., Jeannine Gramick and Robert Nugent, Center for Homophobia Education: New York, NY, 1995, p. 151.

50 "I'm Here," An interview with Andrew Sullivan, *America*, May 8, 1993, p. 7.

51 Cardinal George Basil Hume, *Note on Church Teaching Concerning Homosexual People*, 1995.

8

SJ's Story: "No Better gifts"

"SJ" is 70 years old and the mother of five adult children, two sons and three daughters. Both sons are gay. Raised in a small city in upstate New York, "SJ" raised her own family in that same, seemingly unchanging environment. Though not shocked when her oldest son "came out" to her, neither was she prepared. With honesty and poignancy, she movingly records her journey to understanding.

My older son, Doug, was a year out of college when he told me he was gay. The thought that he was homosexual had darted into my mind occasionally as he was growing up. I would quickly brush aside these thoughts. I was too afraid to even think about the possibility. So, I was not shocked when he told me, but I was terribly worried about what he would have to endure living in a heterosexual world. By this time, he had accepted the fact that he was gay and he was able to be happy. Of course, to arrive at this point in his life, he had had to struggle through times of fear, despair and terrible anxiety. I am sorry that he had to go through that time alone, but I honestly don't know how much help I would have been. Perhaps just telling him that I loved him would have helped.

With Doug's help, I began my journey of learning about the gay community. He introduced me to his friends, took me to Dignity church services (where he was very much involved) and gave me books and other materials to read. He shared what he learned in his scripture study courses. Gradually I came to realize that "gays" and "straights" have *everything* in common—except sexual orientation.

Eventually, he told his sisters. They and their husbands were very accepting. What a relief!

A few years later, my younger son, Joe, told me he was gay as he cried in my arms. He was very unhappy with this realization. I must admit that I was disappointed that *he*, also, was gay. (That's not fair, I thought.) However, it was not a lasting disappointment. I'd had "those years" with Doug and by this time I knew that nothing changes. The relationship you have with your homosexual child is no different than the relationship you have with your heterosexual child. With Doug's help, Joe was able to be at peace with his sexuality.

I am pleased that each son felt he could confide in me. This was not possible with their father, who was not able to accept the homosexuality of his sons. Neither son has his father's support. Doug especially tried very hard to keep open the lines of communication with his father, but he eventually had to give up, as the anguish he suffered with each episode was too much for him. Today, Joe talks to his father only when necessary, but there is no real relationship between them.

My husband and I have been separated for a number of years. Our sons' homosexuality is not the only reason, but his negative reaction to our gay sons was a major factor in my decision to leave him.

I attended a weekend retreat and a day of reflection for parents of homosexual children and found each experience very rewarding. It was exciting to be able to talk openly with other parents. After years of "watching what you say," it was such a relief to be able to talk freely about my homosexual children.

My mother-in-law has never let the homosexuality of her grandsons be a factor in her relationship with them. Even knowing my younger son has AIDS doesn't affect how she treats him. Her love for him is the same as it always was. I think this is remarkable considering her age and the attitude of her son—Doug's and Joe's father. She knows that what matters is the love they have for her and her love for them.

It never occurred to me to talk to a priest when my older son told me he was gay. I was sure I would be told that he was going to hell. I didn't need to hear that.

I am finally finding the courage to speak of my sons' homosexuality with friends. I can relax when I talk of my family. I don't have to always be careful about what I say. I'm hoping my small "one-to-one educating" will be passed on to their families and friends.

I do appreciate the Bishops' statement, *Always Our Children*. However, I don't understand (or agree) that homosexuals must live single lives, devoid of intimacy. We, who are the church, must work to change attitudes. I am discouraged by the Vatican's treatment of Fr. Bob Nugent and Sr. Jeannine Gramick. Parents and families need support especially in the beginning of their journey. I am happy that there are clergy who are compassionate, supportive and understanding. They are most needed. There is so much confusion and fear concerning homosexuals.

I can't end this story without sharing my great joy when Doug and his partner Kurt adopted an infant from Vietnam. Jay is a bright, engaging little boy, the delight of our whole family. He couldn't have two better parents!

I love my sons. I have a great deal of respect for the way they live their lives. I am concerned about the prejudice each must endure and I can't help but worry about the possibility of "gay bashing."

I could not ask for better "gifts" than my children—ALL my children!

9

Parents' Pastoral Voices

In Chapter 7, Casey told how he learned about Catholic teaching on homosexuality. He began with his general understanding that the church said homosexuality is bad—too bad even to talk about. But he knew our son to be a good, deeply spiritual young man so he questioned what he thought he knew and studied church teaching—all of church teaching—as it relates to gay and lesbian people, to sexuality, to justice and to God's love of each person. Casey came to understand that Jim could be gay and Catholic, indeed was gay and Catholic—there was no contradiction.

The thorough, neat and orderly unfolding of Casey's journey belies the messiness of the lived experience of it all, and neglects the frustration, anger and hurt he felt. His story is one of a resourceful, highly motivated person, with the good fortune to have quality educational opportunities at hand where he could explore his questions and concerns. These opportunities are not available to most parents.

While many parents eventually come to the same conclusion Casey did, the confusion and hurt experienced when they learn their child is gay often originates with their child's—and their own—experience of feeling unwelcome in the Catholic Church. How can their children feel welcome when the church calls them "objectively disordered," and says their intimate acts of mutual love are "intrinsically evil?" How does a parent understand this language when they have been taught that each child is God's gift and is loved unconditionally? This chapter will look at parents' attitudes in relation to their faith.

Parents who participated in the survey have very strong feelings about Catholic teaching on homosexuality. These parents attend mass regularly, participate in parish activities and religious education programs, and say their religion is extremely important to them. In similar yet individual ways, they made the same journey as Casey and I, and by their own personal routes, arrived at the same destination—a profound understanding of their gay child simply as a child of God, and God's gift to them and to the world.

The Bible

Two specific questions on the survey —one regarding the Bible, the other about Catholic teaching—offer insight into the reactions of parents to their lesbian daughter or gay son. The first question asks parents to identify passages in the Bible or biblical stories that were either hurtful and confusing, or helpful, in relation to their homosexual child.

Parents were concerned about words like "sodomite," and phrases like "homosexuality is an abomination" and others attributed to the Bible that— sometimes inaccurately—condemn homosexual people. One parent wrote, "There are often cited passages that say homosexuality is sinful—I can't remember chapter and verse—but there are only a few. Yet they are cited enough times to make one think there are many verses."

Casey wrote about the much-quoted biblical texts that are used to condemn homosexuality in Chapter 7. These stories and passages are sometimes called the "Clobber Texts," because they are used to "clobber" our gay children. Indeed, these passages surfaced in response to the survey. Most noted was, Leviticus 18: 22: "You shall not lie with a male as with a woman; it is an abomination" and 20:13: "If a man lies with a male as with a woman, both of them have committed an abomination; they shall be put to death; their blood is upon them." Several commented that these passages are used selectively and specifically to hurt gay and lesbian people with no explanation that these quotes are part of the purity codes of the Israelites, codes which set Hebrews apart from others. (For an excellent presentation read, *What the Bible Really Says about Homosexuality*, by Daniel Helminiak, Alamo Square Press, 2000.)

The story of Sodom and Gomorrah, Genesis 19: 1-25 was frequently mentioned as well. One mother wrote, "It upsets me that some will use scripture to judge others. Some use the destruction of Sodom and Gomorrah as the reason for condemning homosexuals."

Others noted the importance of the historical and social context of a passage or story, indicating that perhaps some of the passages usually thought of as condemning homosexuality might have a different interpretation. This is especially relevant to the story of Sodom and Gomorrah. One parent said, " The story of Sodom and Gomorrah was painful until I understood it related to the sin of inhospitality." Most biblical scholars agree that the "sin" of Sodom was its inhospitality to strangers played out most violently in same-sex rape, which was perceived as the ultimate humiliation of a male.

Some writings of Paul were also felt to be problematic, especially Romans 1:26-27, which speaks of "unnatural acts," but is taken out of the context of pagan idolatry that Paul is recounting.

On the other hand, parents also cited helpful passages and stories from the Bible. These examples most often proclaimed the importance of love. One spoke of Jesus' charge to "love one another" (John 15:17). Another quoted Paul's treatise on love (1 Corinthians 13):

> If I speak in the tongues of mortals and of angels, but do not have love, I am a noisy gong or a clanging cymbal. And if I have prophetic powers, and understand all mysteries and all knowledge, and if I have all faith, so as to remove mountains, but do not have love, I am nothing. . . . Love is patient; love is kind; love is not envious or boastful or arrogant or rude. It does not insist on its own way, it is not irritable or resentful; it does not rejoice in wrongdoing, but rejoices in the truth. It bears all things, believes all things, hopes all things, endures all things. Love never ends. . . . And now faith, hope, and love abide, these three, and the greatest of these is love.

Another parent cited John's description of God as love (1 John 4): "Beloved, let us love one another, because love is from God; everyone who loves is born of God and knows God. Whoever does not love does not know God, for God is love."

Parents mentioned the inclusive nature of God's love, that is, that we are *all* God's children, created from the goodness of God and made in the "image and likeness of God" (Genesis 1:26-27). Many referred to God's love for *all* (their emphasis), and our responsibility to love each other in turn.

Some noted Jesus' proscription against judging others, for example in the story of the woman caught in adultery, when Jesus says to the angry onlookers, "Whoever is without sin, cast the first stone" (John 8: 3-11); and in the Sermon on the Mount when Jesus says, "Do not judge others, and God will not judge you; do not condemn others, and God will not condemn you; forgive others and God will forgive you" (Luke 6:37). Others spoke of God's forgiveness citing the story of the Prodigal Son (Luke 15: 11-32) as an illustration.

The Church

The survey posed to parents the same question in regards to their Catholic faith: What in their Catholic faith was hurtful and confusing, or helpful, in relation to their homosexual child? Again, the responses revealed a mixture of all three: hurt, confusion and help.

Martha, mother of a gay son, articulates the conflict these questions engender. She writes:

My faith, not my religion, has been very helpful on this journey. In the beginning the Catholic Parents Network and Sr. Jeannine [Gramick][1] were very important in helping me feel less alone and isolated. It was comforting to know there are so many of us [parents with gay kids]. But as time goes on, I care less about church teaching. I simply know they are wrong. That's not to say my heart doesn't leap with joy when I hear a priest or bishop say something supportive of the gay community. Today I am very comfortable in the knowledge that God loves my child and his community, that God created him to be gay and wants him to live a full and rich life. I also believe we are chosen to be parents of gay children and we have an obligation to help others understand. Although I am disappointed in my religion for helping to alienate my child and many others who have so much to offer, I readily admit that I am grateful for the Catholic teaching that gave me a powerful faith in God.

I have found nothing in my Catholic *faith* which has been hurtful
or confusing. [But] It is very difficult not to be hurt by my *Church*.

Parents clearly articulated the hurt and confusion they and their children experience at the hands of their Church. They see the Church as judgmental and
condemning of their gay children, and they believe that such judgment encourages prejudice and discrimination which the "so-called 'faithful'" are quick to
demonstrate. This is also evident in "negative preaching" and in the teaching
itself that calls their children "disordered" and "defective." They experience
ignorance, lack of pastoral understanding, inconsistency, confusion, and "outright hostility" sometimes by leadership at the highest diocesan levels. There is
a lack of acceptance and support both for their gay children and for themselves
as parents. In their parishes, they live with a silence that signals either: "We
don't want to be bothered with you," or "This is something so bad, we can't
even talk about it."   In their concern that their gay children have healthy,
happy, holy lives, they question the Church's mandate forbidding sexual intimacy for gay persons; they worry that their child will be condemned to a lonely life. One parent wrote: "Teaching (that) gay people must be [sexually absti-
nent] is unrealistic, undoable, and denies fulfillment of their sexuality."

Conversely, parents found much about their Catholic faith to be quite
helpful. Their Catholic faith helped them know God's "love," "mercy," "compassion," "forgiveness" and "acceptance." Several quoted the teaching in the
Baltimore Catechism (1953), that "God made us to show forth His goodness
and to share with us His everlasting happiness in heaven."[2] And, "To gain the
happiness of heaven we must know, love and serve God in this world."[3] They
praised particular bishops who had been "positive," "gracious," "compassionate," and "sensitive" to gay and lesbian Catholics and their families. Nuns,
priests, and supportive faith communities were raised up as examples of Christ-
like pastoral caring. They affirmed the importance of Church teaching on primacy of conscience and found some hope in the U.S. Bishops pastoral letter,
Always Our Children (AOC). Some were encouraged and sustained by attend-
ing support groups, retreats and workshops offered by various gay/lesbian
parish and diocesan ministries. Finally, they found strength and comfort in
prayer and the sacraments, particularly the Eucharist.

Few parents responded to the question asking if their understanding of
Catholic teaching had changed since they first learned their child was gay, but
certain themes recurred in those few responses. Some found a certain comfort
and support in *Always Our Children* and felt they better understood the full

Church teaching—including primacy of conscience. Others continue struggling with what they see as inconsistencies in the teaching. One parent wrote: "I can't understand. When I went to Catholic school, I was taught to accept and love everyone. Now I find my church can't accept my son as he is." And a few had simply lost all confidence in the church teaching on this matter, one plainly stating "I do not care what the church teaches regarding homosexuality."

Parents' pain is clearly articulated: "I don't think the church thinks about or deals with parents at all. We don't exist to them and there are two of us to every homosexual. We are in deep religious turmoil." But the potential for pastoral response is also evident. There is a clear need for pastoral ministers to address the lack of support, the silence, the confusion and inconsistency, and the ignorance and lack of understanding that pervades our parishes and dioceses. Thoughtful pastoral ministers will attend to the voices of parents articulating what they need from the church and begin discussing how those needs might be met.

Conclusion

I was raised in a strict German-Catholic household and was never even tempted to question Catholic teaching. Still, at age seven, I was distressed by the graves of the babies who were not baptized, buried on the perimeter of the church cemetery—not in the consecrated ground of the cemetery proper. It also bewildered me that intentionally eating meat on Friday was a sin serious enough to merit eternal life in hell—until one confessed. But the Church—as embodied in the nuns who taught me—said it was so, that's all I needed to know. Nevertheless, questions remained tucked away in my heart to be brought out and pondered when I discovered other teachings that didn't make sense if God—as I believed—was all-good, all-merciful and all-loving. For example: my sweet, kind, pious Aunt Ginger married a divorced man and was told she was "out of the church." When the Church called my gay son "disordered," those same feelings stirred. Just as I believe those babies who weren't baptized are with God, I believe that my son is a child of God, "gifted and called for a purpose in God's design."[4] (*AOC*)

In spite of hurtful, sometimes destructive, messages from the institutional Church, Catholic parents find strength in the message of Christ and consolation and sustenance in the sacraments. Love for their child flows from a deep belief in God's love for us all; love for their Church and faithfulness to that

Church springs from an understanding of the Church as the People of God. The Holy Spirit moves in our hearts individually and amongst us as Church as we journey together as "fortunate families."

Notes

1   Sr. Jeannine Gramick was co-founder of New Ways Ministry in 1977 and is active wtih Catholic Parents Network. For more information of New Ways Ministries see the entry for Catholic Parents Network in Appendix C.

2   Father McGuire, for the Confraternity of Christian Doctrine, (1953) *The New Baltimore Catechism and Mass, No. 2 Official Revised Edition*, New York: Benzinger Brothers, Inc., no. 3.

3   Ibid, no.4.

4   *Always Our Children*, p. 4.

10

Len's Letter: "Good Morning, Bishop"

Len and Molly Szumiloski raised their three sons in the finest Catholic tradition: weekly mass (or more often), unfailing observation of Holy Days, Catholic youth groups and regular school of religion for the boys, whole family involvement in parish life. They knew the seasons of the year by the liturgical calendar, not the weather. Theirs wasn't the perfect family—they were smart enough to know that such perfection is a myth. They tackled the same challenges most parents do, and then they tackled one more—when they learned one of their sons is gay. The letter below, written to a Bishop whom Len knew as a parish pastor, clearly articulates the soul-wrenching struggle some parents endure when they learn a child is gay or lesbian. However, the purpose of the letter is not to relate a litany of suffering but to deliver a message of gratitude.

October 30, 1997

Good Morning Bishop,

I am hoping that you remember me from (years ago) when you were pastor of our parish, St. Joseph's, and I was president of the local credit union. You and I had a few discussions in this latter capacity. Sincere, albeit belated, congratulations on your elevation to your post as Bishop. You have our continued prayers for strength and wisdom in your challenging position.

My wife, Molly, and I are so full of joy and happiness as a result of a recent action of the U.S. Catholic Bishops, that we want to express our gratitude not only to God, but to every Bishop we can, and since we know you, we wanted to do so in as personal a way as we can.

I think you may appreciate our renewed Christian joy more if I give you some background about us. Molly and I are daily communicants. I am a lector at daily Mass and once a month on Sundays. We are both Eucharistic Ministers with a special ministry to our local nursing homes where we conduct a weekly Communion Service for the residents. We also assist in our parish CCD program. You may recall that my education included four years with the Jesuits at Holy Cross College. I tell you these facts only to make you aware of the level of our spirituality when an event occurred which changed our lives deeply, dramatically and unalterably: our third son announced to us that he is gay.

This hit us like a "ton of bricks." Our faith was shaken to its roots. It was like the bottom of our world falling out. We felt we were spiraling uncontrollably into the deepest abyss, a feeling of being alone and totally abandoned. We kept asking God why he had done this to us, why he was punishing us, why he had forsaken us. We felt great guilt, that we had done something wrong. And we were sure that the Church's teaching told us that our kind, loving, caring, sensitive, talented, and deeply spiritual son was a sinner, with a blackened soul condemned to eternal damnation. We felt like we were being forced to make a desperate choice, a choice between our Church, which we loved as an integral part of our lives, and our son, whom we loved as a very precious gift from God. We felt guilty for loving our son, thinking God would be angry at us for loving him. This conflict tore at our very being for several years, seriously strained our previously strong marriage, and put me into long and deep depression.

We carried this heavy burden with us for so long, unable to talk with anyone, keeping the heaviness of this secret locked inside. We knew full well what the Catechism said, so we felt there was no point in going to a priest, whom we were sure would only quote to us what we already knew—by heart! We then discovered PFLAG, the very successful secular national support group for parents of gay/lesbian children. We attended several meetings, and although we found some support, it bothered us that prayer or mention of God was not allowed! We wanted—we needed—something more. We wished and hoped that somehow, someday we could find solace through support within our own faith.

Then, like a beacon of light in the darkness, we read that the U.S. Catholic bishops sent out a pastoral letter, *"Always Our Children."* Bishop, you have no idea what effect that letter from you had on us! We couldn't believe it, that our own Church, which we felt had abandoned us to swim in the loneliness of sinfulness, was actually reaching out to us, to give us some consolation, some relief, from the depths of depression to which we had sunk. Your letter "broke the ice" for us. We now felt we could go to our pastor, with whom we discussed the letter. It was then that we discovered that one of your suggestions in the letter, to initiate local Catholic support groups . . . had already been accomplished in our own diocese. The support group is called "Catholic Gay & Lesbian Family Ministry." How spiritually delighted we were that now we could go to a support group which would allow us to pray—to ask for God's help! How great to know that all the Catholic parents going to PFLAG could now come back to a Catholic support group, that the Church wasn't driving them away to a secular support group! This group was sponsoring a retreat for Catholic parents of gay sons and lesbian daughters. Molly and I immediately signed up for this retreat, again so excited that we could find these things within our Church!

Your Excellency, I cannot tell you how the combination of your pastoral letter and that retreat changed our lives. It restored our faith, lit the light once again, filled our hearts with love, brought us peace, and renewed our belief that our Church is the only place to go when life seems to have played us a dirty trick. At the retreat, we found out that many other sincere and devout parents have gone through the very same painful times. Each set of parents got up and told of a slightly different journey of faith through their particular life experience. To hear how the Holy Spirit worked with each set of parents made us realize we were far from alone, and that God had indeed not abandoned us. What a great support we received at that retreat, bolstered by the tremendous love you showed in your pastoral letter to us and to other spiritually hungry Catholics so in need of the Church's help.

The beauty of the experience of the retreat was that it was all done within the framework of our faith, rather than some secular group, and it was surrounded by our Catholic teaching, with prayer and hymns, with emphasis being placed on Jesus' commands: "Love one another;" "Judge not lest you yourself be judged;" and "Whatever you do to the least of my people, that you do unto me." To end the retreat with a Mass, with all of us gathered together to celebrate the Eucharist, was such a beautiful and spiritually uplifting experience! We had been asked to bring a picture of our gay son or lesbian daughter to the retreat; these were placed on a poster board in front of the altar at Mass, with prayerful hope that the grace which flows from the sacrifice of the Mass go for those special intentions. To look up during Mass and see that picture of my beautiful son, being loved by fellow Catholics rather than being condemned, was such a new experience. I am not ashamed to say that I hadn't cried tears of joy for many years, but I did that day. We left the retreat with the weight of the world lifted from our shoulders and a renewed spirit.

The second part of the Catechism's reference to homosexuality, that which deals with the sin of sex acts outside of heterosexual marriage, was quoted and made very clear at the retreat as well as in your pastoral letter. But the emphasis of both was on the first part of the Church's teaching, that which asks us to show love, compassion, and understanding, as Christ would, and not to discriminate or show bias. How spiritually beautiful, and how very much in keeping with Christ's commands! And, I concluded, shouldn't this be our way of treating ALL those whom we think may be sinning, all types of sin? God's message is so simple: Love everyone He has created and leave the judging to Him!

Your pastoral letter's reaching out to Catholic parents such as us seems to now recognize the excruciating emotional and mental pain we have gone through and the need we have had for spiritual consolation from the Church. The content of that letter truly shows a Christ-like guidance and love, not only for us, but also for our gay and lesbian sons and daughters. I firmly believe, I am convinced, that it is actions such as your pastoral letter which move us as a Church one step closer to bringing back those Catholics struggling to understand their sexual orientation, present in them through no choice of their own, and feeling so rejected, lonely and certainly ostracized because of it. I am convinced the Holy Spirit guided you in this work. Thank you, thank you, THANK YOU!

My wife and I will continue to keep you and all Church leaders in our daily prayers. We pray that you and they continue to use as your criteria in all your decision-making, "What would Christ do in this situation? What response best reflects His love?" We also pray that the Holy Spirit continue to guide all of you in leading your flocks, especially in these very difficult times of change (or is it really growth, rather than change??). Lastly, we pray that the Spirit make clear to all of us the difference between what is unacceptable change in substance, and what is acceptable change in the accidents of our faith.

Thank you for taking the time to read my letter and thank you again for the love you have shown. We hope our paths cross again somewhere, sometime. But, meantime, God bless you!

Sincerely in Christ,

Len Szumiloski
(and Molly Szumiloski)

11

Always Our Children

The hope expressed in the letter preceding this chapter encourages a deeper look at *Always Our Children*[1] (*AOC*). Authored by the National Conference of Catholic Bishops' Committee on Marriage and Family, and published in the fall of 1997, *Always Our Children: A Pastoral Message to Parents of Homosexual Children and Suggestions for Pastoral Ministers*:

> . . . is an outstretched hand . . . to parents and other family members, offering them a fresh look at the grace present in family life and the unfailing mercy of Christ our Lord. . . .
>
> Our message speaks of accepting yourself, your beliefs and values, your questions, and all you may be struggling with . . . accepting and loving your child as a gift of God; and accepting the full truth of God's revelation about the dignity of the human person and the meaning of human sexuality.[2]

In general, parents believe this document will be helpful in supporting families and educating faith communities regarding their questions and concerns about homosexuality. Before considering other reactions from parents, let's begin with a theological perspective outlining why parents might feel hopeful about *AOC*.

A theological reflection for "fortunate families" on Always Our Children:
By Casey Lopata

Three principles appear to underlie the wisdom and recommendations of *Always Our Children* that may account for the optimism (90% of parents surveyed) concerning its helpfulness. Ministries that are truly helpful and supportive of Catholic gay and lesbian people and their families are grounded in these three principles: 1) to affirm gay and lesbian persons, as persons; 2) to consider the higher values, not just the rules; and 3) to be consistent when offering pastoral care.

Principle 1: Affirm gay and lesbian people, as persons.

What do you see in your mind's eye when I say "He's gay?" Think about it. Does this conjure up a stereotypical image—the kind the media like to portray when covering a gay pride event? Perhaps a drag queen, or a bare-breasted, "butch" lesbian?

Now what do you imagine when I say, "He's a gay *person*?" For me, that's my son, perhaps dressed in a sport coat and leading the parish assembly in song. "Gay" alone tends to evoke stereotypical images, while "gay *person*" has me searching for a face.

AOC always refers to "homosexual *persons*"—not "homosexuals." For example:

- Every person has an inherent dignity because he or she is created in God's image.[3]

- Concentrate on the person, not on the homosexual orientation itself.[4]

- One's total personhood is not reducible to sexual orientation or behavior.[5]

"Homosexual" is always an adjective, not a noun. Always referring to homosexual or gay or lesbian *persons*, is a subtle but effective way to tell parents that their gay son or lesbian daughter is not an abstract category, not an abstract issue, not a "them;" he or she is a real person with a face and a name.

I wish *AOC* had been available to me back in 1983 when Jim first said, "Dad, I'm gay." One mother expressed this point succinctly:

I know my son. I know who he is, how he was brought up. I know he has a personal relationship with the Lord. How can he—and all the other gay people I know—be what the Church says? That's not who he is.

What she, and I, needed to hear, and what parents need to hear today, is affirmation of our gay and lesbian children as *persons*. Parents need to hear quotes from *AOC* like this:

God loves every person as a unique individual. Sexual identity helps to define the unique persons we are, and one component of our sexual identity is sexual orientation.[6]

And I surely wish *AOC* had been around to tell me I could tell to Jim:

You are always my child; nothing can ever change that. You are also a child of God, gifted and called for a purpose in God's design.[7]

By its tone and its careful choice of words, *AOC* clearly says the starting point for pastoral care with Catholic parents of gay and lesbian people is to affirm the gay son or lesbian daughter as the *person* he or she is—the same *person* the parents have always known.

Principle 2: Consider the higher value, not just the rules.

We need rules. They help us define what abstract values mean. The trick is not to confuse the rule with the higher value. For example, the rule is: don't steal. Yet two Cardinals defended the stealing of food by the poor from supermarkets and warehouses in Brazil with one of them saying, "The Church does not condemn anybody who takes food wherever they find it to avoid starvation."[8] A higher value takes precedence over the rule.

Always Our Children says,

[Homosexual persons], as is true of every human being, need to be nourished at many different levels simultaneously. This includes friendship, which is a way of loving and is essential to healthy human development.[9]

That's why those feelings for Annette Funicello that I talked about in Chapter 7 on Catholic teaching were okay. So, while we can't forget the rules, *AOC* reminds us of a higher value—that friendship is "a way of loving that is essential to healthy human development."[10]

AOC also reminds us to consider the higher value by its definition of chastity:

> Chastity means integrating one's thoughts, feelings, and actions, in the area of human sexuality, in a way that values and respects one's own dignity and that of others.[11]

Most people—heterosexual or homosexual—can defend, even endorse, that definition. We all know the chastity rule—no sexual activity outside of marriage. But by defining chastity in the language of higher values, *AOC* invites us to consider: What does it mean for a person with a homosexual orientation to integrate his or her thoughts, feelings, and actions in a way that values and respects one's own dignity and that of others?

For a long time I focused on whether Jim was following the rules. But that just sidetracked what I really needed to understand: that Jim was the same wonderful person I'd always known, struggling, like we all do, to integrate his thoughts, feelings and actions in a way that values and respects his own dignity and that of others. I echo what one mother we know said about her gay son: "I don't want to love him *despite* his homosexuality. I want to embrace him *as* a homosexual person."[12] Whether we're a parent or ministering with parents, *AOC* encourages us to consider the higher values and not *just* the rules. As *AOC* says: "Christ summons *all* his followers...to a higher standard of loving."[13]

Moral theologian Fr. Richard Peddicord puts this principle into practical terms: "The social participation of gay and lesbian persons is not regulated by the virtue of chastity, but by the virtue of justice."[14] Here Peddicord is less concerned with various types of justice and more concerned with justice as a "univocal" term: "justice does not mean one thing for gays and another thing for straights."[15] In justice, if the Church cannot condemn someone for stealing to avoid starvation, can it condemn someone for seeking "a way of loving . . . essential to healthy human development?"[16] Can we put more restrictions on homosexual friendships than on heterosexual friendships?

Still the rule is there. So what is an appropriate pastoral response when friendship develops into something more than friendship? That leads us to the third principle.

Principle 3: Be consistent when offering pastoral care.

Over and over again, the language of *AOC* calls for consistency.

- God does not love someone any less simply because he or she is homosexual.[17]

- *Everyone*—the *homosexual and the heterosexual* person—is called to personal maturity and responsibility.[18]

- [I]t seems appropriate to understand sexual orientation (*heterosexual or homosexual*) as a deep-seated dimension of one's personality.[19]

- God expects *everyone* to strive for the perfection of love, but to achieve it gradually through stages of moral growth[20].

- With the help of God's grace, *everyone* is called to practice the virtue of chastity in relationships.[21]

AOC is insistent on consistency. Yet how consistent are we in practice? Remember my concern about the likely differences in counseling my married daughter might get regarding birth control (higher values), versus the counseling my son would get regarding homosexual sexual activity (rules)? (See p. 52)

AOC, in essence, says to respect the consciences of gay and lesbian people, just as we should of all people. It specifically tells parents, for example: "[R]emember that you can only change yourself; you can only be responsible for your own beliefs and actions, not those of your adult children."[22]

Consistency, of course, applies to ministry of all kinds. The experience of lesbian and gay people and their parents witnesses a special need. Parents of gay and lesbian children often feel the need to defend their son or daughter, whom they know is a good person, against what seems to be a commonly-held presumption that there is something wrong with their gay child. There seems to be a bias built into society and the Church: when considering morality, being homosexual is less-than being heterosexual. It's as if the gay child is presumed guilty, simply because he or she has a homosexual orientation, and the parent must prove that the child is innocent.

Yet in his book *Gay and Lesbian Rights, A Question: Sexual Ethics or Social Justice*, Peddicord says:

[T]here is no scientific discourse which verifies that punishing instances of discrimination against gay people affects the well being of heterosexual couples and (or) their children. . . . In light of this research, allowing oneself to be guided by the fear that gay rights legislation will sound the death knell for marriage and the family is at least as problematic as opposing the legal availability of contraceptives for the same reason.[23]

If Church ministers employed a consistent pastoral approach, parents would be less likely to feel the need to prove their gay or lesbian child is as good as if he or she was heterosexual. Consistent pastoral ministers can also model for parents how to express love for their gay or lesbian child—a love that is itself "a reflection of God's unconditional love."[24]

To summarize, three basic principles seem to underlie *AOC*: 1) It affirms gay and lesbian people as persons; 2) it considers the higher value and not just the rules; and 3) it offers consistent pastoral care. These principles are characteristic of successful ministry with parents of gay and lesbian people. Ministries that integrate these three principles can help and support gay and lesbian people and their families, and make it significantly easier for parents, and for all of us, to discover the purpose of gay and lesbian people in God's design, and to celebrate how God's love *is* revealed in gay and lesbian people.

Parents' reactions

The Catholic Church has been so silent on homosexuality. The beginning paragraphs of *Always Our Children*, to me, are like a love letter, an outward sign that somebody, anybody, in the institutional Church is listening and has some insight into what we parents know in our hearts and souls about our beloved child. (*One parent's reaction to AOC*)

Casey's theological reflection on *Always Our Children* demonstrates how some parents approach this document. However, in the quote above you can hear both the sadness and the hope with which one parent read *AOC*. Someone in the institutional Church—some bishops—had listened to parents and heard their fear, anger, grief, confusion, isolation, relief, acceptance, protectiveness and love for their gay children. After its publication, if they were still listening, the bishops could hear how parents felt about *AOC*.

If they were listening, bishops would hear expressions of support like, "It validates our love for our child, "It tells parents that 'love' is greater than any institution—church or otherwise," "It gives parents hope for a better life for their children," "It expresses justice and compassion for homosexuals," and "It affirms gay persons saying, 'God does not love someone any less simply because he or she is homosexual.'"

If they were listening, the bishops would have realized that support for the document is often qualified. Although these parents all know Catholic teaching, several were seriously uneasy with the expectation of lifelong sexual abstinence, believing that to be an unrealistic expectation for those not gifted with the vocation of celibacy. They also expressed a deep concern that lifelong celibacy (i.e., sexual abstinence) would mean a lonely life for their child, deprived of human intimacy. Others who believe the document would be helpful had little or no faith that it would be disseminated or implemented on the diocesan or parish level. One parent wrote, "Yes, I think it can help, but I don't think many parents will read it. The bishops put this pastoral message out and they think it is enough. There won't be much dialogue on it." Another parent said, "I think it has already been put aside by most bishops."

The uncertainty these parents feel stems from confusion and conflict created by Catholic teaching on homosexuality. Here are three examples of conflicting messages from *AOC* that might put parents in a quandary:

First, *AOC* states, "Although the gift of human sexuality can be a great mystery at times, the Church's teaching on homosexuality is clear."[25] Parents respond: How exactly can a "great mystery" be so "clear," especially when the voices of those whose lives are being judged are not allowed to be heard?

A *second* area of confusion for parents involves the stressed importance of chastity. *AOC* states that chastity "means integrating one's thoughts, feelings, and actions, in the area of human sexuality, in a way that values and respects one's own dignity and that of others. It is 'the spiritual power which frees love from selfishness and aggression.'"[26] Yet, this definition stands in distinct contrast to other references to chastity in the document which imply unequivocally that to live chastely means total sexual abstinence outside of the married state (which is denied to gay and lesbian couples). Many, including most mental health professionals, would argue that total sexual abstinence (whether inside or outside of marriage) is *not necessarily* a helpful or healthy way for everyone to "integrate their thoughts, feelings, and actions in the area of human sexuality, in a way that values and respects one's own dignity and that of others."

Third, some parents find in *AOC* contradictory statements about the inherent worth of homosexual persons. Sprinkled throughout the document are affirming statements such as: "You are a child of God, gifted and called for a purpose in God's design."[27] "God does not love someone any less simply because he or she is homosexual."[28] "Every person has an inherent dignity because he or she is created in God's image."[29] "One's total personhood is not reducible to sexual orientation or behavior."[30] And "In you [our homosexual brothers and sisters] God's love is revealed." Yet, in spite of these affirming sentiments, when referring to conversion or change therapy, sometimes called "reparative therapy," the bishops say, "Given the present state of medical and psychological knowledge, there is no guarantee that such therapy will succeed. *Thus* there *may be,* [author's emphasis] no obligation to undertake it, though some may find it helpful."[32] There are two difficulties with this statement: first, and perhaps most damaging, is the clear implication that if change is possible, one should change. How does a person recognize and embrace the fullness of who they are as a unique person and a child of God, "gifted and called for a purpose in God's design," when leaders of their Church repeatedly tell them they must (or should want to) change an integral part of who they are? Second, the bishops, while seeming to have educated themselves quite thoroughly on the topic of homosexuality, dismiss or ignore the warnings of the American Psychological Association (supported by virtually all other social science organizations[33]) that there is "no evidence that reparative therapy works, and that it can be quite harmful."[34]

If the bishops were listening they would learn that parents believe *AOC,* helpful though it may be, simply did not go far enough, and had one serious omission. They said:

- "It is a very small step."

- "It still leaves gay people in limbo and parents in a defensive position, vis à vis their children and the Church. Our son, once a strong Catholic, is now very resentful of the Church. He knows we want him desperately to come back but he feels like the Church . . . doesn't sincerely want him and we have a hard time defending the Church in this regard."

- "It opened the doors to discussion instead of division. But it showed the need to go further and admit the human need for physical expression of love."

- And simply, "[It] needs to be stronger, more affirmative."

The hesitancy to give enthusiastic approval to *AOC* relates primarily to one key teaching the bishops neglected to address. That omission: Catholic teaching on the role of personal conscience in moral decision-making. Catholic teaching on homosexuality over the last 25 years has put parents in a place where they feel they must choose between their Church and their child. Some Church authorities might insist this is a false dilemma. However, without a clear exposition of Catholic teaching on conscience, that is precisely the dilemma Catholic parents face.

The Vatican II document *Gaudium et Spes* (Pastoral Constitution on the Church in the Modern World) tells us:

Deep within his [sic] conscience man discovers a law which he has not laid upon himself but which he must obey. Its voice, ever calling him to love and to do what is good and to avoid what is evil, sounds in his heart at the right moment. . . . For man has in his heart a law inscribed by God. . . . His conscience is man's most secret core and his sanctuary. There he is alone with God whose voice echoes in his depth.[35]

Catholic parents who returned the survey and those I've met over the past ten years have with great certainty and passion said that "God's voice echoing in the depths of their souls" tells them that in their gay sons and lesbian daughters "God's love is revealed." These parents know, "Human beings see the appearance, but the Lord looks into the heart."1 Samuel 16:7[36]

If the bishops were listening, they would have heard this good news: the overwhelming majority of parents believe *AOC* will be helpful to families with a gay or lesbian member. It is the most pastoral document on homosexuality yet to come from the U.S. Bishops. Parents say it helps clarify Catholic teaching and dispel some of their misconceptions and it carries weight because it came from the bishops. They believe it indicates a level of pastoral concern and sensitivity that has not been heard from the Catholic Church before. One parent said it this way, "I think the Catholic hierarchy is still in the closet on the very delicate issue of homosexuality. However, with *AOC*, the door to that closet has at least been unlocked."

The bishops have succeeded in taking the initial step of recognizing that families with a gay or lesbian child need and deserve pastoral care. The end of *AOC* lists *Pastoral Recommendations to Parents and Church Ministers*. These are solid suggestions regarding the form such pastoral care might take. In the remaining chapters of this book we'll look at the specific needs of parents and consider these pastoral recommendations in relation to those needs. Who is responsible for disseminating *AOC*, and implementing its pastoral recommendations? Who takes the lead? Are Catholic parents of lesbian daughters and gay sons ready to let the world know of their good fortune?

Notes

1   National Conference of Catholic Bishops, Committee on Marriage and Family, *Always Our Children: a Pastoral Message to Parents of Homosexual Children* (*AOC*). Washington, D.C. 1997, revised with Vatican acceptance, June 1998.

2   *AOC*, p. 1

3   *AOC*, p. 7.

4   *AOC*, p. 6.

5   *AOC*, p. 9.

6   *AOC*, p. 7.

7   *AOC*, p. 4.

8   Cardinal Serafim Fernandes de Araujo of Belo Hoizonettee, and Cardinal Paulo Evaristo Arns, Archbishop of Sao Paulo; *NCR*, May 22, 1998, p. 10.

9   *AOC*, p. 9.

10   *AOC*, p. 9.

11   *AOC*, p. 8.

12   Nancy Mascotte, *NCR*, Sept. 19, 1997, p. 3.

13   *AOC*, p. 8.

14   "Theologian: Church should support gay rights." *Catholic Courier*, Diocese of Rochester, Sept. 24, 1998, p. 3.

15   Peddicord, Richard, *Gay and Lesbian Rights*, Kansas City: Sheed & Ward, 1996, p. 182.

16   *AOC*, p. 9.

17   *AOC*, p. 7.

18   *AOC*, p. 7.

19   *AOC*, p. 6.

20   *AOC*, p. 8.

21   *AOC*, p. 7-8.

22   *AOC*, p. 11.

23   Peddicord, p. 183.

24   *AOC*, p. 5.

25   *AOC*, p. 7.

26   *AOC*, p. 8.

27   *AOC*, p. 4.

28   *AOC*, p. 7.

29   *AOC*, p. 7.

30   *AOC*, p. 9.

31   *AOC*, p. 13.

32   *AOC*, p. 6.

33   Also supported by the American Academy of Pediatrics, American Counseling Association, American Association of School Administrators, American Federation of Teachers, American School Health Association, Interfaith Alliance Foundation, National Association of School Psychologists, National Association of Social Workers, National Education Association, and the American Medical Association.

34   American Psychological Association, "Answers to Your Questions About Sexual Orientation and Homosexuality," APA, Washington, D.C., 1990.

35   *Catechism of the Catholic Church*, # 1776 (1994), quoting "Gaudium et Spes," #16, 1965.

36   *AOC*, p. 7.

12

What Fortunate Families Need

Twenty-eight men and women sat in a circle in the convent meeting room. They were all mothers and fathers of gay sons and lesbian daughters. For all but a few, this was the first opportunity to come together with other parents who shared their experience. The first exercise was designed to help them focus on their gay child and to help them share just a little about that child. A large ball of rainbow-colored yarn—the rainbow colors as always symbolizing hope, but in this instance also indicating the wonderful diversity of God's creation—was given to one parent who said her or his name, their gay child's name, and one thing they wanted the group to know about that child. Then, keeping hold of the end of the yarn, she or he tossed the ball to another parent. That parent, in turn, shared the same three things, held onto their place on the yarn and tossed the ball to another parent, and so on. When everyone was finished they were all connected—by a web made of yarn and by sharing their stories.

There was a second planned part to the exercise, but this group never got to it. Given permission to talk about their gay son or lesbian daughter in a safe and supportive environment, they found it impossible to limit their sharing to only one thing about their child. Each and every parent spoke a litany of the wonderful qualities their gay child embodied. As these parents spoke, a whole new stereotype of gay and lesbian persons was being created. Their gay children—with all their faults left unspoken—were the brightest, most caring and sensitive people in the world.

Tears of relief and joy flooded the circle—relief and joy at finally being able to articulate publicly the goodness of their gay child and their love for that child. Most of the parents at the meeting described above had known their child is gay for years. Yet, that was the first time they had felt safe and accepted; it was their first opportunity for support in a Catholic faith context.

This exercise took place at a day of reflection for Catholic parents of gay sons and lesbian daughters. It shows how isolated parents feel and how much they need to express their love for their gay son or lesbian daughter and share their story with others who will understand.

As noted earlier (Chapter 9), parents make a clear distinction between the invaluable role faith plays in their lives and the—often-unarticulated—need for acknowledgement and affirmation from their Church when they initially learn a child is gay. However, the crucial role of faith and the critical need for support from the faith community do not diminish, but often increase, over time. Many parents draw strength from their faith and the sacraments even while the larger Church, and their parish, lacks awareness of, ignores, dismisses, or denies their need.

Parents find some Vatican documents to be confusing and even quite hurtful. They have great difficulty distinguishing between the philosophical and psychological meanings of words like "disordered." They long for more compassionate and pastorally sensitive proclamations from Rome, but what they want and need most is the support of their local church: their diocese, their parish, the faith community that is—or should be—the loving hand and heart of Christ in their day-to-day lives.

Most parents who felt their faith helpful during the stressful coming out time sought and received comfort and support from religious sisters, pastoral counselors or priests. Still, parents need more than an understanding minister— however important that may be. And it's important to remember the needs of all those parents who avoided their parish pastoral staff—knowing or strongly suspecting that the response would not be helpful. The survey question, "How do you think the Church (that is, priests, sisters, deacons and other pastoral ministers, your faith community and the larger Church) could be more helpful to parents facing this news?" elicited an outpouring of comments from over 170 parents. The passion and candor of their remarks are overwhelming. Over and over they wrote of the need for openness, support, empathetic listening, education—especially for the ministers, and in particular pastors—compassion, an end to secrecy, acknowledgement of their lesbian daughters and gay sons and affirmation of their goodness. Below are a just a few sample comments.

- Education in the spirit of *Always Our Children* is needed. It should be broad-based and required for all teachers and ministers—especially priests. My limited knowledge is more than my pastor's and he's a former high school principal and knows there are many homosexual people in our parish.

- The silence must be broken and people, including parish staff, need to be educated. Parents of gay/lesbian people need to hear them mentioned in prayer.

- Pastoral ministers could be less judgmental, more willing to dialogue and more willing to listen to our life experiences. They could be more welcoming to gay and lesbian persons in that community. The church could also acknowledge the gifts of of gay and lesbian persons who serve the church. They must be filled with rage.

- Stop the secrecy.

- Develop support groups and advertise them—don't keep them secret.

Overall parents' ideas and suggestions fall into strategies that can be translated into meaningful pastoral action. Four general areas of concern emerge from their comments: 1) education, 2) affirmation and reassurance, 3) support and 4) being welcome.

Education

Parents see a critical need for education, for everyone from the pastor and parish staff to the people in the pews. *Always Our Children* recommends that parents "take advantage of opportunities for education and support,"[1] and encourages ministers to "learn more about homosexuality and Catholic teaching so your preaching, teaching and counseling will be informed and effective."[2] Parents add that ministers should be knowledgeable and non-judgmental, able to answer questions, trained as good listeners, open—not secretive. Education is needed at all levels throughout the faith community.

Affirmation and Reassurance

> Sue, a lesbian woman, and her partner, Nadine, have been togeth-
> er for over 15 years. Sue is an architect, Nadine a nurse. A few years
> ago, they adopted a baby girl from China. They literally rescued the
> child from an orphanage unable to care properly for the children.
> Their daughter has the scars which evidence poor care. A while
> back, Sue, Nadine and four-year-old Kelly made a quick weekend
> trip to Florida to celebrate Sue's mother's birthday. While there,
> they all attended Sunday Mass at her mom's parish. As Sue related
> her story, she couldn't hold back the tears when she said the priest,
> in his homily, said that gay and lesbian people were a danger to
> society, and to families in particular—this with her mother and her
> daughter right there. Sue asks, "When is this ever going to end?"

That priest's words wounded Sue and Nadine, but the damage done extends
to their daughter, Kelly, and to Sue's mother, and any other gay or lesbian person or their family members present. Indeed anyone hearing such uninformed,
stereotyping and judgmental words is harmed.

> Peter, was severely beaten outside a gay bar. While he was recov-
> ering from his injuries in an area hospital, he requested a visit from
> his parish priest. The priest refused because the incident happened
> outside a gay bar.

Perhaps incidents like these two are rare—perhaps they aren't—but they represent a reality for some gay and lesbian Catholics and their families. Lesbian
and gay Catholics and those who love them expect to be treated with the dignity and respect due all God's people. At the very least, they deserve to be safe
from such fear-based statements and actions. Indeed, parents deserve to have
their love for their gay child affirmed, and declaration from Church ministers
that God loves their gay child. *Always Our Children* encourages parents to
"accept and love yourselves as parents in order to accept and love your son or
daughter."[4] And it recommends that ministers "avoid stereotyping and condemning. . . [and says to] use the words, 'homosexual,' 'gay,' and 'lesbian' in
honest and accurate ways."[5]

Parents specifically need to know they have done nothing wrong. They
need affirmation from the Church to support the goodness of their child in the
face of discrimination and prejudice from society at large. They need assurance

that their gay son or lesbian daughter is welcome in their faith community, and they need to hear appreciation for the gifts their gay children bring to God's household.

Support Groups

More than half of the parents who said they sought support from people not in ministry went to PFLAG (Parents, Families and Friends of Lesbians and Gays). PFLAG's primary purpose is to support parents when they learn a child is gay. At regular PFLAG meetings parents feel safe to share their fears, confusion, hopes, and joys. They are received with listening hearts, hugs, compassion and understanding. Their children are accepted and affirmed as whole and responsible human beings. Gradually, in such an atmosphere, parents start to let go of their fears and begin a journey to understanding.

Isolation is one of the biggest impediments to understanding and peace faced by parents. Sharing one's story with another who can truly empathize is often the first step to healing. It can be critically important for parents, whose faith is so important, to find a sheltering place within a faith context. *Always Our Children* tells parents to "reach out in love and service to other parents struggling with a son or daughter's homosexuality."[6] It recommends that ministers "help establish or promote support groups for parents and family members."[7] Parents clearly call for support groups, or networks of parents who are willing to share their experience, and to listen to and encourage others. They want support groups formed and places, dates and times of meetings published in Sunday bulletins. They want the secrecy stopped and the stigma of shame lifted. At the very least they need someone to talk to who can relate to their experience.

Welcome

Most parishes claim to be welcoming. But if the very existence of gay people and their families is denied, there can be no welcome for them. Frequently statements like these are heard: "Homosexuality is not an issue in our parish," or "There are no gay people here." If that statement is true in any parish in this country (unlikely), it is because a gay Catholic feels unwelcome, unsafe, unaccepted at her or his core, in that parish—and will remain silent and invisible or leave. It takes no great leap of logic to understand that a parent who loves her/his gay child would also feel unwelcome in such a parish. Welcome can encompass a whole range of attitudes and actions. There are gay and lesbian Catholics who are satisfied if they can partake of the Eucharist at mass and not be overtly shunned or verbally abused from the pulpit. They feel their invitation to the Lord's table is from Christ. For them, it is that simple. For others, it can be much more complicated.

Some feel unwelcome by silence and denial; others feel unwelcome by the perception of subtle prejudice or discrimination. For example: A committed lesbian couple has adopted three children—all half-siblings, the same mother, different fathers. The oldest is five. Nina left her career to care for the children full-time, while Judy shoulders the financial support of the family. Both are "cradle" Catholics who love their faith and need and deserve to be nurtured by the sacraments and a faith community. The family attends Mass each Sunday, and Judy and Nina are as active in parish life as their busy family life permits. Nina is on the parish council, and served as a Eucharistic minister until recently, when she was quietly dropped off the list after a parishioner complained that a lesbian should not be in that role. Neither the pastor nor any of the pastoral staff used the occasion to educate the community. Judy and Nina don't feel welcome in their parish any more.

George, a gay man, states unequivocally that it is not only possible for him to be gay and Catholic, it would be impossible for him not to be. His Catholicism and his gayness are profoundly integrated aspects of who he is. George challenges his own faith community, and by extension, all of us. He says that gay and lesbian people don't want ministry that *simply looks at them as "needy."* George proposes a "strength-based model of ministry," that looks at the whole person—reaching out with healing and support when needed, but also, and perhaps more importantly, knowing, appreciating and nurturing the gifts that gay and lesbian people offer.

The gay man who simply wishes to not be verbally bashed, the lesbian women who want a full, "active role in the Christian community,"[8] and George all really want the same thing: to be loved by their neighbor and loved and judged by God. This is what we all want. Surely we desire support in time of need, but we also need affirmation for the talents God has given us and the energies we bring to our faith community.

To be loved one must first be acknowledged, and that is where a welcoming environment begins. The silence must be broken . . . Parents of gay and lesbian people need to hear them mentioned in prayer. The faith community must condemn obvious homophobic patterns of behavior and belief structures that support it. The community needs to be welcoming in an open and supportive way. And the Church must acknowledge the gifts of gay and lesbian people who have served the Church in the past as well as those who are serving still today—but in silence.

Conclusion

When a faith community is educated, when it offers affirmation to parents and reassurance to their gay sons and daughters, and when it provides support for those who feel confused and isolated, that parish has broken the silence and is on the way to welcoming all.

That knowledge, affirmation, support and welcome will be felt most keenly in families. The family is the arena where most children first find love, understanding, acceptance, support, and affirmation and where they first learn of God's unconditional love for them. And the faith community reaffirms all those values for the child. But as a child discovers she or he is different in this particular way, she or he may no longer assume that the family is a safe and nurturing place and may have picked up signals that the Church is not a safe or welcoming place either. The whole parish community needs to understand, to affirm, to support and to welcome because there are children in every parish, like five-year-old Mike, who is gay, but doesn't know it yet, and seven-year-old Mary, who is lesbian, but doesn't know it yet. If Mike's mom and dad and Mary's mom and dad have experienced a supportive Christian community and have access to resources, when they suspect their child might be homosexual or when they actually hear those words, "Mom, Dad, 'I'm gay." or "Mom, Dad, 'I'm lesbian," they will be able to reach out to their child in love, knowing that they are not alone, that God's all-embracing love is there to draw on and is made manifest in the support of their faith community. They will know that theirs is a fortunate family and that in their child "God's love is revealed."[9]

Notes

1   National Conference of Catholic Bishops Committee on Marriage and Family. *Always Our Children: A Pastoral Message to Parents of Homosexual Children* (*AOC*). Washington, DC, 1997, revised with Vatican acceptance, June 1998. p. 11

2   *AOC*, p. 12.

3   And from a culture that values females much less than males—sometimes, still today, to the point of abandoning female babies.

4   *AOC*, p. 10.

5   *AOC*, p. 11-12.

6   *AOC*, p. 11.

7   *AOC*, p. 12.

8   National Conference of Catholic Bishops (NCCB). *To Live in Christ Jesus: A Pastoral Reflection on the Moral Life*. United States Catholic Conference, Washington, DC. 1976.

9   *AOC*, p. 13.

13

Florence & Steve: "Persons of faith against bigotry"

Florence Balog tells her family's story with loving simplicity and eloquence. Parents of twin lesbian daughters, Steve and Florence exemplify the parable of the servant given many talents: "From those who are given much, much is expected." (Luke. 12:48) They offer a concrete example of what parents can accomplish when motivated by love for their gay children.

My husband, Steve, and I adopted our bi-racial identical twin daughters, Evelyn (Evyn) and Sharon (Ronnie), when they were 5 years old. Their vivacious, creative, compassionate, and resilient personalities drew us to them immediately. We spent lots of time building family: camping, reading, gardening, grieving, crying, communicating, struggling, laughing, playing, building, working, creating, sharing, eating. Together we experienced the hurt of racism, its hatred, ignorance and discrimination, as well as its physical violence. They were our children and we loved them.

During their high school years we began to sense that our daughters might be lesbian. They did not date boys or go to dances. They left literature by and about lesbians around the house. Like many teenagers, they were often moody, irritable and confused, and had difficulty communicating. We sensed they might be afraid we'd reject them. Finally, when they were 20 years old, I decided to pose the question, hoping to open the way for communicating.

So one day on a shopping errand with Ronnie, I looked at her hesitantly and said, "Ronnie, are you lesbian?"

She looked at me silently. Then smiling from ear-to-ear, dark eyes sparkling, she said, "Yes, Mom!" The "secret" between us was gone and we both sensed relief. When I later shared the "news" with Steve, he wasn't surprised.

The next day Evyn, who was in the army, called from Fort Jackson, S.C. and said, "I hear Ronnie came out to you guys!"

I replied, "She did. And are you lesbian, too?"

"How did you know, Mom?" And over the miles of telephone lines, the relief in Evyn's voice was palpable.

Ronnie said she had been extremely fearful and frustrated when she thought about coming out. She believed society would reject her. She had heard of so many kids who had been thrown out of the house, dropped by friends, challenged and insulted by strangers and ignored in social settings. She also feared that in coming out, she would shatter our dreams for her and felt the dreams she had for herself would be even more difficult to achieve. She wondered, too, what our response would be.

Steve says that when our daughters came out to us the thought of rejecting them never occurred to him—nor did the thought of denying them or changing them in any way. It was evident that this was not something they were choosing, but was simply a realization by them and a revelation by them of who they were and their basic, intrinsic sexual orientation. They were our daughters just the way they were! And we loved them that way!

All four of us felt relief; however, Steve and I also felt uncertain, confused and fearful about what all of this meant both for them and for us. Accepting our daughters' sexual orientation was one thing; integrating that knowledge into our beings and our relationship with others was another. We found ourselves "feeling outside", "on the edge", always as if we "had something to hide." We were reluctant to share this information with friends, neighbors, parishioners, fellow workers, and especially, our relatives back "home" in the Midwest. We were unsure about how they would accept it. For five years we inhabited a dreadfully lonely, silent place.

During those five years, Steve and I were fearfully apprehensive of the picture society and the media gave of homosexual persons. Our daughters did not fit that picture. They were very normal young women. We were confused by the fact that we experienced our daughters as wonderfully warm, loving, compassionate, vivacious young women. How could people hate and discriminate against them for being who they were? We were confused also by the strangely silent stance and seeming condemnation by the Catholic Church. Neither one of us had ever heard a homily in which homosexual persons were named and included among those that Jesus loved. We felt completely outside of our circle of friends and our church, unable to find support from these two groups that had been the forming influences of our lives.

One question that continued to plague me during these years of silence was: "Why can't I affirm my wonderful daughters?" When relatives, friends, parishioners, and neighbors asked, "How are your daughters? Do they have boyfriends yet?" or "Are they married yet?" or "What are they doing now?" I would often avoid the issue by replying, "Oh, they're doing their thing, you know!" Each time I said that, I would feel a slight "tug" inside, reminding me that I wasn't being completely truthful.

The silence within me was squirming and I began to look to my parish for some kind of support. Two things happened. The first was mention, in our Sunday church bulletin, of an article entitled, "Homosexuality: Challenging the Church to Grow" by John McNeill. (*The Christian Century*, March 11, 1987). I felt that was what I needed to do: challenge the church to grow and openly accept my daughters and call them by name. I felt a road had opened up for me and that I was going to walk down that road.

Second, I met a member of our church who was wearing a button—a pink triangle with the words, "Person of Faith Against Bigotry." I told her my story. Tears welled up in both of us. I had broken my silence! I had shared my deep, dark secret. She looked at me with the utmost understanding and compassion and said, "And you were not able to tell anyone here at our parish about it." I said, "No!" On the spot, we decided our parish needed to openly welcome gay, lesbian, bisexual, and transgendered persons. Our diverse parish had already done much work on discrimination and racism and it was "ripe" for welcoming homosexual Catholics.

Steve joined us in asking our pastor to form a committee to explore ways in which our parish could become more welcoming. With our pastor's support the "Welcoming the Whole Family Committee" was begun. Surprisingly twelve parishioners showed up for the first meeting. I felt we were "on the road," with support from each other. It was a wonderful feeling for Steve and me. We were no longer alone.

Over the next four years, our committee became very active. We didn't really have a plan, but relied on the Spirit to lead us along the way. We felt we were in uncharted territory. We began by educating ourselves and studying church documents on the subject of homosexuality. We went on to set up a library of resources in our parish; present parish adult education classes on sexuality, homosexuality, and scripture; survey parishioners' attitudes towards homosexual persons and their participation in our worship; hold a parish Town Meeting providing an opportunity for discussion of parish hopes and fears; present a diocesan-wide workshop on the Bishops' letter, *Always Our Children*. We also wrote a welcoming statement which is now on the front of our Sunday Parish Bulletin. It says that our parish "*is a faith community baptized into one body, which honors and celebrates diversity. We welcome and include persons of every color, language, ethnicity, origin, ability, sexual orientation, marital status, and life situation.*"

As parents Steve and I also communicated with our congressional representatives at the national, state, and local levels on issues affecting our daughters. We wrote letters to members of the Catholic hierarchy in support of our daughters. We wrote letters to the editor of our local newspaper, as well as our diocesan paper. We contributed toward signature ads in the *New York Times* and the *National Catholic Reporter* in support of our gay/lesbian ministers and to express our alarm over hate crimes against gay/lesbian persons. We wrote a letter to our local chapter of PFLAG in support of our Catholic ministers who were silenced by the Vatican. The Welcoming the Whole Family Committee thrives and has evolved into a Small Faith Community. The support we received from this church-based group exceeds any of our expectations.

While we work to make our parish community more welcoming, our daughters' feelings about the church's attitude toward them because of their sexual orientation are clear. They both feel alienated and unwelcome. Evyn says she no longer believes in the Catholic Church. She finds it "bigoted, hateful, and hypocritical." She says she definitely has a spiritual life outside the church and believes in God's inclusive love, but does not see the Church reflecting Christ's love. She has the same aspirations and goals as anyone else and hopes some day to make a permanent commitment to another person she loves. She says, "My life is based on honesty and truthfulness. Hatred, bigotry and fear create deceit. I live with a firm belief in myself and the love and acceptance I experience within the lesbian/gay community."

Ronnie says that as a young minority woman, she was already struggling within society before she came out. She sometimes has a difficult time functioning in society as a bi-racial woman. "I didn't want to also be a lesbian," she said. "I didn't want to have one more difference that could be used against me." She says she has feelings of loneliness and alienation from the church. "Religious rhetoric has lost sight of the great commandment." She considers the church to be hypocritical. "It is trying to force me to be against myself —to live between truth and lies. It's so confusing," she says. She relates that she has a strong spiritual life and tries to keep it simple, "Treat other people as you want to be treated." She does not see the Church doing that. "I see the Church giving support to those who choose to hate and judge. I am so tired of hearing brainless rhetoric about the negative things the Bible says about homosexuality."

At times our daughters ask us why we are doing what we're doing to explore ways to make our church and society more accepting. We tell them, "Because we love you and because of the injustice so many like you are experiencing. Christ's love for all includes you, by name." Meanwhile, the Church continues to tell them they are "disordered" and that in a loving stable permanent relationship sexual expression of their love for each other is "intrinsically evil". This is not the Jesus they know. This is not the Church they choose to believe in. They know who they are, God's creation, and that "It is good!" As Evyn says, "God don't make no junk!" Both have suffered physical assaults, mental and emotional abuse because of their sexual orientation. They continue to be confused by the rejection for being who they are.

Our 30-something daughters have breathed new life into their 60-something mother and father. We love them just as they are, and are so grateful for the challenges and opportunities to celebrate and experience diversity, and to fight for justice. We, our parish, and our society, are more enriched and enlightened because of who our daughters are.

14

Strategies for Pastoral Care

. . .[M]y gay and lesbian brothers and sisters, you have told me over years in conversations with you . . . that far more often than not, our faith community seems forbidding; that in it you feel unwelcome; that your own struggles, issues, questions, joys, sorrows, talents, needs, gifts, are not respected as they should be. I hope I can say with confidence that this gathering this afternoon symbolizes a widespread sentiment among the people of our diocese, that we'd like to do a better job on that. And we would like to convey to you in a ... rewarding and genuine way, the respect that we have for your integrity, your goodness and your gifts. And ...we... say to you with equal honesty that we are the weaker to the degree that we do not enjoy the wonderful gifts God gives you for the sake of the community. So may I ask you please to forgive us for all the ways, witting and unwitting, that we have failed to honor and respect you.

Bishop Matthew Clark
March 1, 1997

At 2 o'clock in the afternoon on March 1, 1997, Bishop Matthew Clark processed into Sacred Heart Cathedral in Rochester, NY. He was greeted by the voices of over 1200 gay and lesbian Catholics and their families and friends singing "All are welcome in this place." That moment and the Eucharistic celebration that followed are forever etched in the hearts of all who were there. Years of prayer and listening and learning had preceded Bishop Clark's courageous pastoral decision to offer the reconciling embrace of the Eucharist to gay and lesbian Catholics and all those who love and care for them.

This story illustrates what prayer, perseverance and patience can produce. Five years earlier, Catholic Gay and Lesbian Family Ministry (CG&LFM)— composed of three religious sisters, three lay people (including Casey and myself), and two priests—had come together committed to finding a way to more fully welcome our gay and lesbian sisters and brothers into the Church of their baptism.

Initially the group had no clear idea what they could do. They had a few brainstorming sessions over dinner but were still searching for a way to get some gay/lesbian ministry started when an opportunity presented itself from an unlikely source. In July 1992, the Vatican Congregation for the Doctrine of the Faith issued to U.S. Bishops a document titled, "Some Considerations Concerning the Catholic Response to Legislative Proposals on the Non-Discrimination of Homosexual Persons." One can imagine the hurt and anger generated by statements like the following:

> There are areas in which it is not unjust discrimination to take sexual orientation into account, for example in the placement of children for adoption or foster care, in employment of teachers or athletic coaches and in military recruitment.[1]

These words give the impression that Church authorities not only believe, but are also ready to promulgate, stereotypes that insist that gay men are pedophiles and that lesbian women and gay men are somehow dangerous to children and in some way unworthy to serve in their nation's military. Gay and lesbian Catholics were not willing to sit silently and be thus slandered. They wrote letters and called chancery offices. In Rochester, NY, Bishop Matthew Clark responded in his weekly column in the *Catholic Courier*. He proposed to "hold conversations about these sensitive issues with Catholics who are homosexual persons so that we might deepen mutual understanding in order that when we disagree we might do so with respect, so that we can continue together on our common journey of faith."[2]

Knowing many lesbian and gay Catholics, CG&LFM could arrange for and facilitate such a meeting for Bishop Clark. The planned meeting was simply an opportunity to honestly talk with and respectfully listen to each other. Bishop Clark heard the pain and anger and witnessed the alienation felt by lesbian and gay Catholics in the Rochester Diocese. Although no particular actions developed from that meeting, together participants experienced the hurt and hope, love and limits that we all share in ministry with lesbian and gay persons. Each participant recognized and understood that the Holy Spirit would work in and through all of those elements, and that abundant faith and vast reserves of patience would be necessary before gay and lesbian Catholics would be welcomed unconditionally in the Church they love.

CG&LFM came away from that encounter aware of the serious need for education—especially education of the whole faith community. We developed a workshop series on moral discernment in relation to homosexuality, using the classic, four-part model of moral decision-making—scripture, tradition, reason and experience. That workshop, available to any parish or group, is the core work of CG&LFM. The other major focus of the group is support for Catholic parents of lesbian daughters and gay sons—offering annual days of reflection, meetings in parishes and a phone line to call just to talk.

In September 1996, CG&LFM entered into a collaborative relationship with the Rochester Diocese. Its mission statement reads:

> Catholic Gay and Lesbian Family Ministry, on behalf of the Diocese of Rochester, advocates for and facilitates pastoral care for Catholic gay and lesbian persons, their families/households, and their friends. Our guide for this ministry is the U.S. Bishops' pastoral letter which says: "Homosexual [persons], like everyone else, should not suffer from prejudice against their basic human rights. They have a right to respect, friendship, and justice. They should have an active role in the Christian community."[3]

This account of how CG&LFM got started, along with the story of Florence and Steve Balog, parents of the twin lesbian daughter (Chapter 13), are but two examples of how pastoral care for lesbian and gay Catholics can become reality. In the process of building the ministry and by meeting and comparing experiences with others, CG&LFM drew up a list of strategies that may be useful to develop an environment that is welcoming for lesbian and gay Catholics.

Strategies to help gay & lesbian people & their families feel welcome in your parish

1. *Ensure general hospitality for all.* How hospitable is your parish—for anyone and everyone? If the general parishioner does not feel welcome, someone on the margins of the Church surely will not feel welcome.

2. *Break the silence and continue to send signals. Always Our Children* says: "When speaking publicly, use the words 'homosexual,' 'gay,' and 'lesbian' in honest and accurate ways." Use of these words by persons in leadership roles gives permission for others to talk about gay and lesbian loved ones and related issues. It may be just the signal someone in need of pastoral care is looking for. Another signal is putting *Always Our Children* and similar literature in the church vestibule. Send those signals often and in many ways. People often don't see or hear even the clearest signals until the need becomes important for them.

3. *Ensure consistency.* How does your parish treat divorced and separated people? Divorced people who have remarried without an annulment? Unmarried, cohabiting heterosexual couples—young or old? People with spouses who are not Catholic? Are lesbian and gay people, individual or couples, and their families treated the same as others who may feel marginalized by the Church? Or is there a double standard?

4. *Focus on the person.* Lesbian and gay people are not an "issue." Use "gay" or "homosexual" only as adjectives. Say "gay and lesbian persons," not "gays and lesbians." Put a face on it. If people are willing to be "out," find ways to let them tell their stories.

5. *Listen.* Understand objections. Discern what is lack of information (which requires education) versus irrational belief (which requires a change of heart). Make an extra effort to listen to people who believe they're not being heard.

6. *Be honest.* This can be extremely hard when your arguments are falling on deaf ears, yet you believe what you're working for is right. Try not to overstate your case, e.g. on the causes of sexual orientation, or the percentage of the population that is gay.

7. *Don't confuse issues.* Focus on inclusion as your goal and don't be distracted by other issues. For example, some of your allies may want to work to change Catholic teaching. If that is not kept separate, it will become THE issue and inclusion will fall by the wayside. There's plenty to do within the bounds of Catholic teaching.

8. *Work with allies.* Who else doesn't feel welcome? What about divorced and separated people? Racial or ethnic minorities? Young people? Anyone else who feels different? What can be done in common with others who feel marginalized? What about friends in other faith traditions or secular organizations? Allies can also help you through those times when the going gets tough.

9. *Don't reinvent the wheel.* Don't copy blindly but—if it can work for you—borrow unashamedly what others have done. Give credit where due, and always ask for permission when appropriate.

10. *Be patient.* Our local ministry's overall strategy can be summed up in the motto: "You just never know!" In one sense that means you never know who is lesbian or gay or who has a loved one who is. So, we're always sensitive to that possibility. It also means, no matter how insignificant an effort seems, how few people it seems to reach, or how unresponsive your audience appears, you never know who you've touched in some way that will make a difference—perhaps years from now.

No parish can say, "We don't need to deal with 'that' issue. There are no gay people in our parish." Such denial creates silence around homosexuality that, in turn, increases the sense of isolation for both the gay person and his/her family members.

When Catholic parents feel fear for their child, and confusion and grief regarding their child's homosexual orientation, can they feel comfortable approaching their parish professional staff for pastoral care? Some feel comfortable; others do not. Those who don't, may fear being blamed, may fear their child will be judged and condemned, or may simply be too embarrassed to verbalize their feelings. Yet parents who sought support from parish ministers or pastoral counselors were quite satisfied with the help they received. More than half said their encounters with ministers and pastoral counselors were "very helpful." Perhaps those priests, religious sisters and pastoral counselors gave subtle clues that they were understanding. Or perhaps the parents who went for such help intuitively sought empathetic persons. Maybe these pastoral ministers understand the grief and the fears of those parents. Such pastoral ministers have a unique opportunity not only to support grieving parents but also to open dialogue with the whole faith community with solid educational programs.

Reaching out to lesbian and gay Catholics and their parents can be as simple as providing copies of *Always Our Children* in the parish literature rack, or as elaborate as the development and implementation of an inclusive, welcoming mission statement like the Balogs did in their parish. (Chapter 13, p. 101.)

Each parish will approach pastoral ministry with lesbian and gay Catholics and their families in a way that uses the particular strengths and talents of the parish to meet the its particular needs. An example: Several years ago, St. Mary's Parish in Rochester, NY offered a Lenten program that dealt with the fact that we all suffer in various ways and often need to reach out for help. One week the program consisted of a panel of ordinary parishioners simply telling their stories. An older man spoke of his loneliness after his wife's death the year before. A young couple told of their profound grief at losing two children to miscarriage in the first few years of their marriage. A middle-aged couple described the frustration and exhaustion that comes from caring for a family—and each other—over many years. And finally a lesbian woman spoke of her "coming out experience." This last speaker's story was a revelation to those who heard it and many were moved to tears. But the hidden story behind this story has three major points: 1) this lesbian woman trusted at least one person on the pastoral staff with her story; 2) that staff person responded to her in a pastorally sensitive way; 3) the pastoral staff agreed that, if the woman was willing, the whole faith community would benefit from hearing her story.

Within a year, that woman along with a small group of lesbian and gay parishioners started a support group. The met in homes, spreading the news of the group by word of mouth. After a while they put a notice in the Sunday bulletin and invited anyone interested to come to a meeting in the rectory. The group was called St. Mary's Support Group for Gay and Lesbian People. When non-gay people started coming, "Families and Friends" was added. The format of the meetings was to begin with prayer and then hang out and chat about what was going on in their (our) lives including current frustrations—often with the Church; to seek advice about "coming out" issues; sometimes to comfort a hurt or grieving person; and to occasionally share good news. Basically it was a group of new and old friends just being there for each other—which was great, but after a year or so it began to fall apart—some of the leaders had moved away and much of the conversation became repetitive. Eventually only the leaders were showing up, so an emergency meeting was called.

Three important decisions were made at that emergency meeting: *first*, the group would continue—if only because it was so important to have that notice in the bulletin twice each month. People who saw that announcement knew gay and lesbian people were welcome at St. Mary's—whether they cared to attend the meetings or not. *Second*, the name of the group needed to be changed. The sense was that people didn't need another "support group," and there was some discussion that perhaps some people might think the group wanted to support them out of their so-called "lifestyle." And so, the group became St. Mary's CONNECTION for Gay and Lesbian People, Families and Friends, which was both pastoral and inclusive. *Third*, components of education, prayer and service were added to the already- established community element. So, to the occasional potluck dinner and movie night were added an annual service project, a yearly spiritual day of reflection and four educational forums each year.

For several years the new format worked and the whole parish community was enriched by the educational offerings. But inevitably, the leadership grew weary and interest waned—not unlike other volunteer groups that ebb and grow over time. But in the meantime, gay and lesbian people had become fully integrated into the life of St. Mary's parish—from Eucharistic minister and lector to committee member and Parish Council member. So, while active formal ministry with lesbian and gay people is sometimes elusive at St. Mary's, the parish lives a vision of what a welcoming parish is.

At another parish, a pastor who, over the course of a few years became aware of several couples in the parish who had gay children, initiated a support group for parents who might like a chance to meet with other parents, to talk about their experiences and concerns. There was considerable anxiety that meetings not be disrupted by persons who were not parents of gay children, but who felt driven to set the group "straight," so to speak. A poignant article by the pastor in the Sunday bulletin (see Appendix F), telling of his experience with gay Catholics and their parents announced the formation of a group that would meet monthly. Interested persons were to call him for more information. This was to welcome and assure those who might be nervous about coming to a group, and also served to screen those who might prove to be disruptive. Initially the group limited its outreach to parishioners only, but after about six months, the invitation was sent to neighboring parishes. The parents who were the group leaders were closeted outside of the group and this made outreach difficult. Being closeted also creates an environment of fear and shame, and while these are understandable feelings for those still struggling, if the leadership has not been able to work through these feelings, the group will be at a severe disadvantage.

Another support group for parents was started when a mom approached her pastor and asked if such a group could meet in their church hall. He said "yes," and then it was up to this mom and her husband to make it a reality. It took lots of time, energy and perseverance: planning where and when to meet, publicizing the meetings locally and in the diocesan news, planning how to deal with potential trouble and, perhaps hardest of all, sticking with it when only one or two people showed up for months on end. Four years later, that group not only has survived, but has grown and now that diocese has a place where parents can safely meet to share their fears and their joys. (See Appendix C for NACDLGM)

The survey results clearly indicate that there are knowledgeable and sensitive priests, sisters and pastoral counselors. These ministers can be a core of support and education for other pastoral ministers throughout their diocese. They should be encouraged to share their knowledge, skills and insights with pastoral ministers—professional and lay—in other dioceses throughout the country. The National Association of Catholic Diocesan Lesbian and Gay Ministries (NACDLGM) is an organization that can help ministers by: (a) discussing strategies for starting a pastoral ministry with lesbian and gay Catholics and their families; (b) identifying resources; and (c) networking, to share ideas for outreach, support, and education.

Outreach, support and education in relation to homosexual persons and their families can be difficult to start, primarily because of the fears mentioned above, but also because of the controversial nature of homosexuality in today's society. In 1999, the then-President of the National Conference of Catholic Bishops, Joseph Fiorenza said, "Homosexuality is such a sensitive issue in our society that an outreach and ministry to homosexual persons, even when carried out in accord with Catholic teaching, can still be subject to misunderstanding and criticism, [perhaps resulting in hesitation] to engage in this outreach at all. . . . The Congregation [for the Doctrine of the Faith] clearly does not want such a result."[4]

Such outreach cannot begin at the parish or diocesan level until the silence is broken. Only then, can supportive outreach to families with gay and lesbian members and educational forums for all parishioners about sexuality and homosexuality be developed. Breaking the silence can happen in many different ways. For instance, prayer leaders and homilists can say the words *homosexual, gay, lesbian,* and can include gay and lesbian people when praying for or preaching about those who are oppressed or discriminated against.

Untold good would unfold if every diocese provided a copy of *Always Our Children* to each and every pastoral minister and encouraged them to take whatever steps—big or small—they could to implement the pastoral recommendations. This recalls one specific concern of parents, i.e. that this document will never be disseminated or implemented. Extra effort may be necessary to see that, at the very least, copies of the pastoral letter are made available to anyone in any parish who is interested. Every pastoral caregiver in every parish should be familiar with *Always Our Children*. This pastoral message deserves careful and sensitive reading and study by the whole faith community. It is important for them to hear words like these from *Always Our Children*:

- It is not sufficient only to avoid unjust discrimination. Homosexual persons 'must be accepted with respect, compassion and sensitivity.'[5]

- Nothing in the Bible or in Catholic Church teaching can be used to justify prejudicial or discriminatory attitudes and behaviors[6].

- God does not love someone any less simply because he or she is homosexual.[7]

Always Our Children challenges the whole faith community to live the gospel values of love and justice. Parents can simply ask someone on the pastoral staff to order copies of *Always Our Children* and to see that they're available in the back of church. With such a simple request, a parents may find themselves beginning the process of ministry in their area—becoming lay ministers for other parents who look to them for support, education, guidance and hope.

Professional ministers, too, can benefit from hearing their stories, listening to their pain and their joy.

As a long-range goal, every diocese can develop and implement a ministry—based on the suggestions and pastoral recommendations in *Always Our Children*—that supports families of gay and lesbian Catholics, educates the entire faith community on issues related to sexuality and moral discernment within the Catholic Church, and ultimately results in a respectful, welcoming environment for all God's children.

I end this chapter with a vignette that shows what a welcoming parish looks like.

> Kurt and Doug were meant to be dads. Doug is a special education teacher. Care and empathy ooze from every word and gesture. Kurt works for a large corporation and has an irrepressible spirit. His love and joy in life are infectious. They met at church where Kurt was singing in the choir and Doug was a liturgical minister.
>
> After being together for ten years, they decided it was time to take the next big step: they wanted to adopt a child. They prayed, talked, and studied and, after much research, decided to adopt a child from Vietnam. Despite the typical frustration and stress involved in the process, things were moving along quite nicely. Doug, as the legal adoptive parent, was told they were to get a little girl. They received a picture and gave their daughter a name. Two months before they were to get her—as friends were preparing a baby shower—they were notified that the adoption agency in Vietnam was bogus and their child was no longer available. Their family and friends rallied 'round them as they mourned their loss. Kurt and Doug were determined to move forward and several-months later they went to Vietnam and brought back their son, five-month-old, "DJ."
>
> The first Sunday that Kurt and Doug brought "DJ" to church, the pastor publicly welcomed the child to the community and announced that there would be a special blessing after mass for anyone who had adopted a child, was adopted themselves, or was in any way touched by the miracle of love that adoption signifies. At least fifty people stayed for that blessing. After the blessing, a number of Kurt's and Doug's gay and lesbian friends stayed for a

group picture. The picture of their adopted children looked like a United Nations of children. Children, black, white and all shades in between, were from Colombia, Hungary, China, Vietnam, and the U.S. Thus, "DJ" was warmly welcomed and a few months later was baptized at Sunday Mass, with a married couple and a priest as Godparents. You can be sure that the whole faith community affirms the gifts of this "fortunate family."

These young men come from "fortunate families" . . . and everyone knows it. Doug is the son of "SJ" whose story is in Chapter 8. Everyone in his family loves and affirms Doug and his son, "DJ." Kurt's parents are supportive, too. Kurt's grandmother—DJ's great grandmother—looks forward each summer to seeing Kurt, Doug, and especially DJ at their mountain cottage. Recognition of the good fortune of our families, and a willingness to share that good fortune, that good news, with all whose lives we touch, will sure-ly change the world.

Notes

1   Congregation for the Doctrine of the Faith (CDF), *Responding to Legislative Proposals on Discrimination Against Homosexuals* 1992, # 11.

2   Bishop Matthew Clark, "Letter's Intent is Misunderstood," *Catholic Courier*, Rochester, NY, August 20, 1992, p. 2.

3   National Conference of Catholic Bishops (NCCB), *To Live in Christ Jesus: A Pastoral Reflection on the Moral Life*, USCC. 1976, # 52, and (NCCB), *Human Sexuality: A Catholic Perspective for Education and Lifelong Learning*, U.S. Catholic Conference, 1991, p. 55.

4   Bishop Joseph Fiorenza, "NCCB President Calls for Acceptance of Church Teaching on Homosexuality." *USCC NEWS*, USCC Website, July 13, 1999.

5   National Conference of Catholic Bishops (NCCB), Committee on Marriage and Family, *Always Our Children (AOC)*. U.S. Catholic Conference, Washington, DC, 1997, revised June 1998, p. 9.

6   *AOC*, p.10.

7   *AOC*, p. 7.

15

Conclusion:
In US God's Love is Revealed

A Fortunate Daughter's Story

I have loved God all my life. I have walked with Jesus in the center of my being for as long as I can remember. I had my first formal "taste" of Eucharist when I was seven years old, but I encountered Eucharist long before that. My mom, grandparents, aunts, uncles, and later, my stepfather instilled in me a love for Eucharist as we sweated, laughed, cried, prayed, grew tired, working long hours together in our family vineyard. To break open our lives, tell our stories, hold each other, offer drinks of cold water from the well that soothed our aches and tempered our weary bodies, to pray that "God stand in the space between us . . ." (My Gramp's favorite line from scripture) were common experiences that kept us loving even during difficult transitions and losses. God always loved me through my family. That faith has sustained me.

Church was also part of our family life. We went to Mass on Sundays and Holy Days. We prayed the rosary together on Wednesday evenings and listened to Grandpa read from the Bible every night. I was led to believe that my Church needed me, and I needed the Church if I were to be whole. That belief has been challenged since I was ten years old.

"Queer" was the only word I had to describe something I felt at the age of ten. My mom had used it in reference to young men she knew. I asked her what the word meant and she told me it described men who cared for each other instead of being attracted to women. I held that word for two weeks before I asked Mom if women could be "queer" too. She said simply, "I suppose so." Oh, I felt like dancing. Her words calmed something in me. For the next two weeks, I was somewhat reflective, but on a search. I talked to my friends to see what they knew. One of my friend's mothers said that it was wrong for two girls to kiss each other. "God doesn't like girls to do that," she said. Anyone who did would end up in hell, she proclaimed. I will never forget the afternoon of my next encounter with Mom and this word "queer." While Mom was reading the newspaper, I asked her if it was bad to be queer. Lowering the newspaper just a bit, Mom's hesitant voice queried, "Why do you ask?" My response was a typical ten-year-old's carefree response: "Because I might be one." Hiding behind her paper, I heard Mom say, "Well, if you *are*, then that couldn't be bad, right?" "Right," I responded and walked away from that afternoon feeling whole. I was comforted that day in 1956. Incidentally, I never really felt such comfort or hope again until 1997, when I read the words: ". . . you are always our children." I wept that day because few embraces of my whole person have been given to me, especially from my Church.

~ Mary

Mary's mother revealed God's love by affirming not only the goodness of her daughter, but the goodness of her daughter's lesbianism. When we affirm our gay children so unequivocally we also reveal God's love and assert that our family is indeed fortunate. I believe we must assert that affirmation beyond our gay sons and our lesbian daughters and beyond our family. We must tell the world of the good fortune of having a "two spirited" son or daughter.

Telling the world isn't always easy. When Jim came out to me, I knew I didn't feel good, and I knew I had to turn to God. Fear, anger, and painful isolation sometimes overwhelmed me, but I knew having a gay son wasn't the end of the world. Even when the pain subsides, we can get beyond "cross to bear" thinking and rejoice in our good fortune. Henry Nouwen, in an essay entitled *Drinking Our Cup* writes,

> "Making the best of it" is not what drinking the cup is about. Drinking the cup is not simply adapting ourselves to a bad situation and trying to use it as well as we can. Drinking our cup is a hopeful, courageous, and self-confident way of living. It is standing in the world with head erect, solidly rooted in the knowledge of who we are, facing the reality that surrounds us, and responding to it from our hearts.[1]

Having a gay son or lesbian daughter is not an experience we must "make the best of." It is an encounter with a reality that calls forth hope and courage, a reality that calls us to respond from our hearts. The stories in this book attest to that reality.

Asked if their relationship with their gay child had changed since the time they learned of their child's orientation, virtually all parents who acknowledged a change declared that the change was for the better. They were much closer to their child, their relationship was more open, honest and caring. These families recognize how fortunate they are.

Parents of "special" children, whether they are challenged in some specific way or particularly talented, often come together to find strength and wisdom and to help each other make the world a better place for their children and all children. Parents of gay sons and lesbian daughters can do no less. If, indeed, we believe we are "fortunate families," how can we not inform the larger world of our good fortune? Each parent must find his or her own way to make a difference, because each parent, each child, and each family is unique. But each parent *must do something*.

- Talk to your child.

- Ask if she or he is comfortable with you "coming out."

- Reach out to one other person, to give comfort, to receive wisdom, to share your good fortune.

- Challenge the offensive remark or joke.

- Start a support group.

- Educate yourself.

- Educate others.

- Go on a retreat.

- Plan and offer a retreat for others.

- Get to know lots of gay and lesbian people; get to know their parents

- Talk to your pastor, your religious education minister, your bishop.

- Write a letter.

- Write a book.

- **Do something to let the world know about Fortunate Families!**

Always Our Children proclaims to our gay children, "In you God's love is revealed." When parents take action, God's love is revealed in and through *us*.

I started this chapter with the story of a lesbian woman—in her own words—because we so seldom hear the voices of our lesbian daughters and gay sons; even less do we publicly hear parent's unequivocal love for them.

I close with the words of a gay man, our son Jim. In 1998, the National Association of Catholic Diocesan Lesbian and Gay Ministries held its annual conference in our city. For the Mass that ended the conference, Jim wrote a meditation song. The lyrics relate, with poignancy and hope, the journey of spiritual growth we all travel. As members of Fortunate Families we are all made in the image of God.

IMAGE OF GOD[2]

When I was a child, I thought as a child.
I gazed at the heavens, and danced in the mud.
I was who I was, a creation of God,
Knew not foolish from wise,
I saw with God's eyes:

> *Refrain*:
> Image of hope, Image of love,
> Image of joy and peace and justice,
> Image of faith, Image of grace,
> Image of glory, Image of God.

As I grew up I was taught who to be,
What to do, when to speak, who to love, how to see.
I saw things with new eyes, but something was wrong.
In the midst of it all, I forgot this true song:

> *Refrain*:
> Image of hope, Image of love,
> Image of joy and peace and justice,
> Image of faith, Image of grace,
> Image of glory, Image of God.

Now I am an adult, not a child any more.
I seek the great visions I know from my youth.
Let God's love be my teacher, and conscience my guide.
When the world looks at me,
I hope that they'll see:

> *Refrain*:
> Image of hope, Image of love,
> Image of joy and peace and justice,
> Image of faith, Image of grace,
> Image of glory, Image of God.

James Lopata

Notes

1   Henri Nouwen, (1998) *Selected Writings*, New York, Orbis Books, p. 31.

2   James Lopata, for the Eucharistic Liturgy, *Imaging Justice*, NACLGDM 5th Annual Conference, Rochester, NY September 1998. Used with permission.

Bibliography

American Psychological Association (APA), *Answers to Your Questions About Sexual Orientation and Homosexuality*. Washington, DC. 1993, and 1998.

Blumenfeld, Warren J. *Homophobia: How We All Pay the Price*. Boston: Beacon Press. 1992.

Borhek, M. V. *Coming Out to Parents: A Two-Way Survival Guide for Lesbians, and Gay Men and Their Parents*. Cleveland, OH: Pilgrim Press. 1993.

U.S. Catholic Conference. *Catechism of the Catholic Church*. 1994.

Catholic Bishops of Scotland and Wales, Catholic Welfare Commission. *An Introduction to the Pastoral Care of Homosexual People: Pastoral Guidelines for Priests*. 1979.

Congregation for the Doctrine of the Faith (CDF). *Letter to the Bishops of the Catholic Church on the Pastoral Care of Homosexual Persons*. CDF. 1986.

CDF. *Responding to Legislative Proposals on Discrimination Against Homosexuals*. 1992.

"Clark Plans Mass for Homosexuals." *Democrat and Chronicle*. Rochester, NY. Feb. 19, 1997.

"Letter's Intent is Misunderstood." *Catholic Courier*. Rochester, NY. August 20, 1992.

Constitution on the Church in the Modern World (Gaudium et Spes). Vatican II, December 1965.

Dew, Robb Forman. *The Family Heart, A Memoir of When Our Son Came Out*. New York: Addison-Wesley Publishing Company. 1994.

Griffin, C., Wirth, M., and Wirth. A. *Beyond Acceptance: Parents of Gays Talk About Their Experiences*. New York: St. Martin's Press. 1986.

Helminiak, Daniel. *What the Bible* Really *Says about Homosexuality*. New Mexico: Alamo Square Press. 2000.

Hetrick-Martin Institute. FACTFILE: Lesbian, Gay and Bisexual Youth. Referencing Remafedi, G., "Male homosexuality: the adolescent's perspective." *Pediatrics*, 79. 1987.

Holy Bible: New Revised Standard Version. New York: Oxford University Press. 1977.

Hume, Cardinal George Basil. *Note on Church Teaching Concerning Homosexual People*. 1995.

John Paul II. *Crossing the Threshold of Hope*. New York: Alfred A. Knopf. 1994.

Karol Wotyla (Pope John Paul II): An Anthology. Edited by Alfred Bloch and Gerge T. Czuczka. New York: Crossroad. 1981.

McNaught, Brian. "Reflections of a Gay Catholic," in *Homosexuality and the Catholic Church*. Jeannine Gramick, ed. Chicago: Thomas More. 1983.

National Conference of Catholic Bishops (NCCB) Committee on Marriage and Family, *Always Our Children, a Pastoral Message to Parents of Homosexual Children and Suggestions for Pastoral Minister. (AOC)*. Washington, D:, U.S. Catholic Conference. 1997, revised 1998.

NCCB. *To Live in Christ Jesus: A Pastoral Reflection on the Moral Life*. Washington, DC: USCC. 1976.

New Baltimore Catechism and Mass, No. 2 Official Revised Edition. Father McGuire, for the Confraternity of Christian Doctrine. New York: Benzinger Brothers, Inc. 1953.

Nouwen, Henri. *Selected Writings*. New York: Orbis Books. 1998.

Nugent, Robert and Jeannine Gramick. *Building Bridges: Gay & Lesbian Reality and the Catholic Church*. Mystic, CT: 23rd Publications. 1992.

Pius XII. *Address to Midwives*. 1951.

Pontifical Council for the Family. "Vade Mecum for confessors Concerning some Aspects of the Morality of Conjugal Life." *Origins*, March 13, 1997.

Roberts, Tom. "He's Not Disordered. He's My Brother." *National Catholic Reporter*. Nov. 4, 1994.

Sabol, G. *Gender and Religiosity: Do These Factors Influence Parental Attitudes Toward A Homosexual Daughter or Son?* Dissertation: Loyola College, Maryland. 1996.

Sullivan, Andrew. "I'm Here, An Interview with Andrew Sullivan." *America*. May 8, 1993.

Switzer, David K. *Coming Out As Parents, You and Your Homosexual Child*. Louisville, KY: Westminster, John Knox Press. 1996.

U.S. Catholic Conference. *Human Sexuality: A Catholic Perspective for Education and Lifelong Learning*. 1991.

Untener, Bishop Kenneth E. "Hallmarks of the Church" [Address delivered at New Ways Ministry Symposium, March 28, 1992], in *Voices of Hope*. Eds. Jeannine Gramick & Robert Nugent. New York: Center for Homophobia Education. 1995.

Visser, Jan, quoted by Sean O'Riordan, C.Ss.R., in "The 'Declaration on Certain Questions concerning Sexual Ethics': A Discussion," James McManus, C.Ss.R., Sean O'Riordan, CSs.R., and Henry Stratton, *The Clergy Review*, London, June 1976, v. 61, no. 6.

Williams, Walter L. *The Spirit and the Flesh: Sexual Diversity in American Indian Culture*. Boston: Beacon Press. 1992.

Appendix A:
A Survey of Catholic Parents with Lesbian Daughters and Gay Sons 1998

Demographic & Family Information
(*Note: If you have more than one child who is homosexual, answer the questions about the first one you learned about.*)

1. Your birth date _____

2. Your ethnic background:
   Race_____ Nationality _____

3. (circle one)   Female   Male

4. Your highest level of education: (check one)
   __ less than high school graduate
   __ high school graduate
   __ some college but less than bachelor's degree
   __ bachelor's degree
   __ graduate study

5. How many children do you have?_____
   How many are homosexual? _____

6. Your responses to this survey will be about a:(circle) son   daughter

7. Is this child your: (circle) biological child   adopted child

8. If biological, are you currently married to this child's other biological parent? (circle)   YES   NO

9. If adopted, are you currently married to the spouse with whom you adopted this child? (circle)   YES   NO

10. When did you find out your child was homosexual? Year _____

11. Your age when you found out _____

12. Your child's age when you found out _____

General Reaction

13. How did you first learn of your child's homosexual orientation? (check all that apply)
    __ Face-to-face with her/him
    __ By phone from him/her
    __ In a letter from her/him
    __ From another family member
    __ From non-family member
    __ I figured it out by myself
    __ Other _____

14. In general, how would you evaluate your initial emotional reaction when you learned of your child's homosexual orientation? (circle where you fall on the scale) positive   1   2   3   4   5   negative

15. As well as you can remember, how did you respond to your child? What did you say and do? (If you need to use extra paper, indicate the number of the question you are answering.) _____

16. Which of the following describes your feelings when you learned your child is homosexual. (check all that apply):
    __ fear (for your child)
    __ fear (for yourself)
    __ understanding
    __ shame
    __ loneliness/ isolation
    __ protectiveness
    __ anger
    __ confusion
    __ relief

___ shock
___ acceptance
___ denial/disbelief
___ guilt
___ embarrassment
___ grief
___ other _____

17. At the time you learned of your your child's homosexual orientation, which of the following might have described your understanding of homosexuality? (check all that apply)
    ___ Homosexuality is a choice.
    ___ Homosexuality is caused by dysfunctional family dynamics, e.g. domineering mother and distant father.
    ___ Homosexuality is genetically determined.
    ___ Homosexuality is immoral.
    ___ Homosexuality is unnatural.
    ___ Homosexuality is an illness, like alcoholism.
    ___ Homosexuality can be cured, i.e. homosexual people can be changed to be heterosexual.
    ___ Homosexuality is natural for some people.
    ___ Homosexuality is a "defect," similar to a physical handicap, like blindness.
    ___ Homosexuality is an "imperfection" like color-blindness.
    ___ A homosexual orientation is not sinful but homosexual genital behavior is.
    ___ Other _____

18. At the time you learned of your child's homosexual orientation, which of the following describes your understanding of Catholic Church teaching about homosexuality? (check all that apply)
    ___ Homosexuality is morally wrong.
    ___ A homosexual orientation is not sinful, but any homosexual genital activity is sinful.
    ___ Our sexuality, whether homosexual or heterosexual, is a gift from God.
    ___ A life of total sexual abstinence is required of all homosexual persons.
    ___ Other _____

19.How did you feel about that teaching as you understood it? (check one)
___ strongly agree
___ agree
___ neither agree nor disagree
___ disagree
___ strongly disagree
___ don't know
___ don't understand the teaching

20. Before you learned of your child's homosexuality, did you personally know anyone else who was homosexual? For example: a friend, neighbor, or co-worker? (circle)   YES   NO

21. Before you learned of your child's homosexuality, were you aware of anyone else in your immediate or extended family who was homosexual? For example: brother/sister, cousin, aunt/uncle, grandparent. (circle)   YES   NO

22. Today, what are your greatest concerns about having a homosexual child? (check all that apply)
___ the prejudice of society
___ he/she will go to hell
___ he/she will live a lonely life
___ people will reject him/her
___ he/she may lose his/her job
___ family reaction
___ he/she will never have children
___ AIDS
___ gay bashing
___ other _____

23. Have you told any of your friends that you have a homosexual child? (circle)   YES   NO

Religious Framework

24. Were you? (circle)
Born and raised Catholic   Adult convert to Catholicism

25. How often do you go to Mass? (check one)
___ not at all
___ once or twice a year
___ monthly--on average

___ weekly Sunday mass
___ more often than weekly
___ other _____

26. Do you participate in other church activities? For instance: social or service organizations, prayer groups, etc. (circle) YES NO

27. Did you attend parochial school? (circle) YES NO
    If so, for how many years? _____

28. Did your homosexual child attend Catholic school? (circle) YES NO
    If so, for how many years? _____

29. Have you ever attended an adult education program in your parish or diocese? (circle) YES NO

30. In general, how important is your religion to you? (circle where you fall on the scale)

    Extremely important   1   2   3   4   5   not important at all

31. How would you describe your attitude regarding religion? (circle where you fall on the scale)

    Very traditional   1   2   3   4   5   Very progressive

32. How do you feel about the church's teaching on the following subjects?
    1 = strongly agree; 2 = agree; 3= neither agree nor disagree; 4 = disagree; 5 = strongly disagree; 6 = don't know; 7 = don't understand the teaching: (circle where you fall on each scale)
    a. artificial birth control: 1   2   3   4   5   6   7
    b. masturbation: 1   2   3   4   5   6   7
    c. primacy of conscience: 1   2   3   4   5   6   7
    d. social justice: 1   2   3   4   5   6   7

33. Do you read the bible? (circle one) Never Rarely Sometimes Often

34. If there are any particular biblical passages or stories that you find helpful in relation to your homosexual child, please give an example.
    _____

35. If there are any particular biblical passages or stories that you find hurtful or confusing in relation to your homosexual child, please give an example. _____

36. What, if anything, in your Catholic faith have you found helpful in relation to your homosexual child? Please describe in as much detail as you can ._____

37. What, if anything, in your Catholic faith have you found hurtful or confusing in relation to your homosexual child? Please describe in as much detail as you can. _____

38. If your understanding of church teaching has changed since you first learned of your child's homosexual orientation, please explain in what way it has changed and why you think it has changed. _____

Pastoral Support

39. When you learned of your child's homosexual orientation: (circle the number)

	Very much			Not at all	
a) Was your Catholic faith helpful?	1	2	3	4	5
b) Was your Catholic faith an obstacle?	1	2	3	4	5
c) Did you feel a need for support (someone safe to talk to)?	1	2	3	4	5
d) Did you need accurate information about homosexuality?	1	2	3	4	5
e) Did you need accurate information about church teaching about homosexuality?	1	2	3	4	5
f) Do you still feel the need for support and information?	1	2	3	4	5
g) How important is it that you get that support and information from the Catholic church?	1	2	3	4	5

40. If you approached any of the following for support or information, check (3) which one(s) and indicate the level of helpfulness by circling the number. (check all that apply)
    a priest:
        Very helpful   1   2   3   4   5   not helpful at all
    a religious sister:
        Very helpful   1   2   3   4   5   not helpful at all
    pastoral counselor:
        Very helpful   1   2   3   4   5   not helpful at all
    did not approach any of the above.

41. If you did approach one of the above for support, in what way was it helpful or not? _____

42. If you were not comfortable going to the church for support, did you seek support elsewhere? (circle)   YES   NO
If yes, where did you seek support? _____

43. How do you think the church (that is, priests, sisters, deacons and other pastoral ministers; your parish faith community and the larger church) could be more helpful to parents facing this news? Please be as specific as possible. _____

44. Have you read *Always Our Children*, the U.S. Bishops' pastoral message to parents of homosexual children and suggestions for pastoral ministers? (circle)   YES   NO
If yes, do you think that document will be helpful to other parents with homosexual children? (circle)   YES   NO
Please elaborate: _____

45. How comfortable are you with people knowing you have a homosexual child? (Circle where you are on the scale.)
very comfortable   1   2   3   4   5   very uncomfortable

46. Has your relationship with your homosexual child changed much in the time since you learned of his/her orientation? (circle)   YES   NO
If yes, how?_____

47. Have your religious beliefs been instrumental in that change? (circle)
YES   NO
If yes, how? _____

Appendix B:
Survey Results

This research project was developed to collect data regarding Catholic parents' reactions to their gay sons and lesbian daughters. The project also addresses how these parents' Catholic background has influenced that reaction and how they feel the church can be helpful to gay and lesbian Catholics and their parents. The survey was organized in four parts: *demographics* to describe the population responding; *general reaction* to identify the feelings and understandings of parents when they learned of their child's homosexual orientation; *religious framework* to establish the relative importance of their Catholic faith in their lives as well as to identify areas that may indicate conflict with teachings of the church; and *pastoral support* to determine what parents need in the way of ministry support. A total of 760 survey packets were sent to Catholic parents with gay or lesbian children and church ministers who work with gay and lesbian Catholics and their families.

Demographics

More demographic data were collected than needed to address the survey's purpose. Some of this information may be helpful in future studies. The data shown here describe the target subjects who responded to the survey.

Two hundred ten surveys were returned. (Note: Not every person answered every question so totals do not always equal 210. Percentages are based on the number who answered a given question, so n = number of people who responded) The demographic data collected show virtually no diversity of race or national origin with only five respondents indicating other than "white" or "Caucasian" and European ancestry. Those five classified themselves as "brown" and of Mexican background.

The survey was returned by 157 females and 52 males, with one not answering this question (see Table 2). Of the gay children, 155 were sons and 53 were daughters (see Table 3).

Table 2: **Survey Respondents by Sex** (n = 209)

Father	52 (25%)
Mother	157 (75%)

Table 3: **Sex of Gay Child of Survey Respondent** (n = 208)

Son	155 (75%)
Daughter	53 (25%)

Of the gay children, 13 were adopted. The number of children in a family ranged from one to nine, with most families having two or three children. Twenty-nine of the respondents have two gay children and three respondents have three gay children. Three-fourths of the respondents were married to the gay child's other biological parent and 12% made a point of saying they were widowed (that is, they wrote it in).

Respondents' ages ranged from 40 to 89 (see Table 4). The age at which parents learned of their child's homosexuality ranged from 36 to 86 with the majority learning in their 50s (see Table 5). The ages of the gay sons or lesbian daughters when their parent learned of their homosexuality ranged from 11 to 49, with most coming out between 18 and 30 (see Table 6).

Table 4: **Age Range of Survey Respondents** (n = 210)

Age Range	Number
40-49	5
50-59	74
60-69	92
70-79	27
80+	12

Table 5: **Age of Parent When He/She Learned of Child's Homosexuality** (n = 207)

Age Range	Number
less than 40	3
40-49	56
50-59	101
60-69	40
70-79	7

Table 6: **Age of Child When Parent Learned of His/Her Homosexual Orientation** (n = 206)

Age Range	Number
11-17	18
18-30	158
31-39	24
40-49	6

Respondents' educational level ranged from less than a high school level to graduate-college study (Table 7).

Table 7: **Educational Level of Respondents** (n = 209)

Level of Education	Number (%)
less than high school graduate	7 (3%)
high school graduate	51 (24%)
some college, less than Bachelor's degree	52 (25%)
Bachelor's degree	37 (18%)
Graduate study	62 (29%)

General Reactions

Questions asked in this section deal with the parents' feelings and their understanding of homosexuality at the time they learned a son or daughter was gay. How did they find out? What is their assessment of their reaction? What do they remember of their child's coming out to them? How did they feel? What did they understand about homosexuality? How did they understand church teaching on homosexuality? Did they know of any friends or relatives who were gay? What were their greatest concerns? And finally, as an initial indicator of their comfort level, they were asked if they had told any of their friends about their gay son or daughter.

Of the 210 parents who responded, 130 (62%) learned of their child's homosexual orientation directly from their gay child. Sixty parents (29%) said they had figured it out by themselves.

Question 14 asked parents to rate their reaction when they learned of their child's homosexuality. Question 15 then asked them to relate as well as they could remember what happened, what they said, how they responded.

Table 8 shows the percentages and raw numbers of how parents rated their initial reaction when they learned of their child's homosexual orientation.

Table 8: **Parents' Assessment of Their Initial Reaction to Their Gay Child** (n = 203)

1 (Positive)	2	3	4	5 (Negative)
21 (10%)	22 (11%)	66 (33%)	43 (21%)	51 (25%)

Some of the comments written to Question 15 underscore the subjective nature both of their feelings and their assessment of those feelings. For instance, one mother evaluated her initial response to her daughter as "very negative" but, when describing what happened, she wrote: "I told her I loved her, and asked if she is sure, and is she happy with her decision. That's what's important." Another parent who ranked himself "very positive" quoted himself saying to his son: "It's your life and you have to live with it," a statement some would not describe as "very positive."

Examples of comments from parents who rated their reaction as "positive:"

- I will never forget the awful pain I heard in our child's voice when he said, 'I'm gay, Mom.' I said, 'I love you. We love you. Remember how we have always told you, you were planned for and a wanted child.' As I hung up the phone I remember saying to myself, 'God help us all.' When my husband got home I took both his hands in mine and said, 'I have something very big to share with you. David has called and I heard the pain in his voice and he is telling us he is gay.' We hugged each other, talked some more and called our son back and both told him together how much we loved him.

- I hugged her and told her I loved her more than ever and if that was who she is, just please be moral in that lifestyle, as we would expect her to be if she were heterosexual.

Examples of comments from parents who rated their reactions "somewhat positive:"

- I answered my daughter's letter telling her I loved her very much and her homosexuality . . . will require more of my love and concern, rather than less.

- I responded pretty well. Was not shocked, I had felt something was going on in his life, but was not sure what it was. His father and I told him we loved him . . . we wanted him to continue coming home and being a part of the family . . . We did not want any secrets between us as we were a close family . . . The next morning was very different, his father was ready to sell the house and move out of town, he was never going to tell anyone . . . But the bottom line was that we loved our son and his siblings loved him as well. We knew we had to educate ourselves.

Sample statements of parents who rated their reactions neither positive nor negative, or both negative and positive:

- (I was) anxious to know why. Was it my fault? How did he feel?

- I asked if he was sure. We cried together. I told him I loved him and asked many questions about how he felt growing up. I tried to be supportive of his emotional needs, though I felt devastated myself.

- I just sat there! I didn't know what to say. As she continued talking, past occurrences seemed to fit together and my immediate reaction was to feel very hurt because she had not trusted me enough to say anything before.

Samples of comments from parents who rated their reactions "somewhat negative:"

- Initially (I) was shocked/saddened/disappointed. I tried to be reassuring to our son. We never felt negative toward him. We did convey we would always be there for him, that would never change.

- I was accepting and kind; but deep inside very sad and disappointed. I told him I had suspected it. In 1987, he was hospitalized for suicidal tendencies. This was his second time to be hospitalized for this. His doctor called me at work and asked me if he was gay. I responded by saying, "I hope not." He asked, "why?" I said because of making life so hard for him. The doctor didn't tell me he was gay, so I still tried to deny it.

Sample comments from parents who rated their reactions as "negative:"

- Like most of us, I was in total shock and cried, almost uncontrollably for many days. I said many things I shouldn't have, but I'm not sure it could have been any other way--I was so unprepared and unsuspecting. I was angry, at him, at God for letting this happen to us. I felt like it must be a mistake, that maybe he had it wrong. I thought we must have had something to do with it. Since our son has always prided himself on not following the crowd, on being a little different, I thought maybe he was just doing this to be different. We never withdrew our love or wanting him to be part, a close part, of the family. It's that we had to process so much and fit the pieces of the puzzle that is our son back together.

- (I) was shocked and abused him by calling him names. He left in anger but my wife convinced me to remember his excellent behavior and absolutely wonderful record... After an initial outburst of anger, I suggested that we could have him changed. However, he said, "No, I don't want to try that." The very next day we told him that we loved him and we would do anything we could to help him.

- I will always love the sinner, but not the sin.

Table 9: **Parent's Initial Feelings When Learning of Their Child's Homosexual Orientation** (n = 209, respondent could check as many as applied)

Feeling/Emotion	Number (%)
fear (for your child)	162 (78%)
confusion	118 (56%)
grief	103 (49%)
protectiveness	98 (47%)
acceptance	89 (43%)
guilt	82 (39%)
shock	73 (35%)
loneliness/isolation	72 (34%)
embarrassment	69 (33%)
understanding	66 (32%)
denial/disbelief	57 (27%)
anger	56 (27%)
shame	52 (25%)
fear (for yourself)	42 (20%)
relief	28 (13%)
other: sadness, anxiety, concern, love, ignorance, pride, disappointment, empathy, powerlessness	26 (12%)

Table 10: **Parent's Fears and Concerns for Their Homosexual Children** (n = 202, respondent could check any that applied)

Fears/concerns	Number (%)
The prejudice of society	184 (92%)
People will reject him/her	129 (64%)
AIDS	95 (47%)
He/she will never have children	75 (37%)
He/she may lose his/her job	69 (34%)
He/she will live a lonely life	65 (32%)
Family reaction	51 (25%)
Gay bashing	21 (10%)
He/she will go to hell	15 (7%)
Worried about the church's negative attitude toward their homosexual child.	7 (3%)
Other	24 (12%)

Table 11: **Parent's Understanding of Homosexuality When They Learned of Gay Child** (n = 210, respondent could check any that applied)

Statement about homosexuality	Number (%) agreeing
Homosexuality is unnatural	85 (40%)
Homosexuality is genetically determined	82 (39%)
Homosexuality is natural for some people	78 (37%)
A homosexual orientation is not sinful, but homosexual genital behavior is	71 (33%)
Homosexuality is immoral	61 (29%)
Homosexuality is caused by dysfunctional family dynamics: e.g. a domineering mother and distant father	52 (25%)
Homosexuality is a "defect" similar to a physical handicap, like blindness	33 (16%)
Homosexuality is a choice	29 (14%)
Homosexuality can be cured, i.e. homosexual people can be changed to be heterosexual	24 (11%)
Homosexuality is an "imperfection" like color-blindness	21 (10%)
Homosexuality is an illness, like alcoholism	12 (6%)
Other: ignorance mentioned most often	47 (22%)

Table 12: **Parent's Understanding of Church Teaching Regarding Sexuality/Homosexuality** (n = 202, respondents could check as many as applied)

How church teaching understood	Number and %
Homosexuality is morally wrong	125 (62%)
A homosexual orientation is not sinful, but any homosexual genital activity is sinful.	68 (39%)
Our sexuality, whether homosexual or heterosexual, is a gift from God.	29 (14 %)
A life of total sexual abstinence is required of all homosexual persons.	87 (41%)
Other	26 (13%)
Number of "other" who wrote in "ignorance" or " unawareness" of church teaching regarding homosexuality.	15 (7%) of total

In Question 17 parents were given a list of brief statements about homosexuality and asked to check each statement that fit their understanding of homosexuality—at the time they learned their child was gay. Table 11 shows their responses. When asked about their understanding of church teaching at the time they learned of their child's homosexual orientation, parents responded as shown in Table 12. Of the parents who responded, 70% personally knew someone else who is homosexual, and 32% were aware of a gay family member (see Table 13).

Table 13: **Parents Who Knew Someone Gay When Their Child Came Out to Them**

Personally knew a gay/lesbian person	Knew of another gay family member
(n = 201) 140 (70%)	(n = 200) 63 (32%)

Finally, as a measurement of their comfort level with having a homosexual child, parents were asked if they had told any of their friends about their gay child. Only 169 (80% of the total respondents) answered this question. Of those, 148 (88%) said "yes."

Religious Framework

This section asked questions calculated to assess respondent's level of religiosity, their commitment to and immersion in the rituals of the Catholic church as well as their exposure to church teaching and their understanding of it. Open-ended questions asked for specific examples of biblical passages and church teachings that were helpful, or hurtful or confusing to the respondent in relation to their homosexual child. On most multiple-choice questions, parents were asked to mark all that applied, and in open-ended questions, they could incorporate more than one idea or feeling. Therefore, few of the percentages add up to 100%.

Importance of Catholicism

Of parents responding, 183 (91%) were born and raised Catholic, 18 (9%) were adult converts to Catholicism. When asked how often they attended mass, 180 (80%) said they went to mass weekly or more than weekly, including 14 (7%) who attend mass daily or almost daily. A total of 23 (11%) said they attended mass monthly (on average), once or twice a year, or not at all. Of those, 7 said "not at all," 2 of them explaining, "Until the church welcomes my son for who he really is, I won't go," and " I won't return till the church welcomes my son. We used to go every Sunday." Of those responding, 173 (86%) said they participated in other church activities such as service activities, or social or prayer groups; and 152 had attended an adult education program in their parish or diocese (see Table 14).

Table 14: **Level of Religious Involvement of Parents Responding**

(n) Religious Activity	Number (%)
(n = 203) Mass weekly or more often	180 (89%)
(n = 203) Mass less than weekly	23 (11%)
(n = 200) Other church activities	173 (86%)
(n = 201) Adult Religious Education	152 (77%)

As one indicator of their immersion in and commitment to the Catholic faith, parents were asked if they or their child attended Catholic school. One hundred and four (52% of those who answered this question) had attended Catholic schools four years or more; 109 (54%) of the gay children referred to had attended Catholic schools four years or more; 41 (29%) of the parents who went to Catholic school did not send their gay child to Catholic school; and 30

(50%) of the parents who did not attend Catholic school sent their child to Catholic school.

To the question, "How important is your religion to you?" on a 5-point scale with 1 being extremely important and 5 being not important at all, parents answered as shown in Table 15 below.

Table 15: **Importance of Their Catholic Faith in the Lives of Respondents** (n = 199)

1 (Extremely important)	2	3	4	5 (Not at all important)
147 (74%)	28 (14%)	10 (5%)	5 (2.5%)	9 (4.5%)

Respondents ranked their own attitude regarding religion as shown in Table 16.

Table 16: **Respondents Describe Their Own Religious Attitudes** (n = 200)

1 (Very traditional)	2	3	4	5 (Very progressive)
18 (9%)	13 (6%)	47 (24%)	51 (26%)	71 (35%)

Table 17 shows respondents attitudes toward four specific church teachings: artificial birth control, masturbation, primacy of conscience, and social justice. Respondents were asked to rank their attitude toward church teaching on each of those topics on a scale of 1 to 7 with 1 = strongly agree; 2 = agree; 3 = neither agree nor disagree; 4 = disagree; 5 = strongly disagree; 6 = don't know; and 7 = don't understand church teaching.

Table 17: **Respondent's Agreement with Church Teaching on Four Issues**

	1	2	3	4	5	6	7
Birth Control (n = 199)	13 (6%)	19 (9%)	33 (17%)	48 (24%)	83 (42%)	1 (.5%)	2 (1%)
Masturbation (n = 196)	14 (7%)	15 (8%)	43 (22%)	31 (16%)	53 (27%)	31 (16%)	7 (5%)
Primacy of Conscience (n = 192)	62 (32%)	49 (25%)	17 (9%)	7 (4%)	6 (3%)	21 (11%)	30 (16%)
Social Justice (n = 193)	61 (32%)	68 (35%)	20 (10%)	5 (3%)	6 (3 %)	19 (10%)	14 (7%)

Table 18 shows the agreement and disagreement on those issues by respondents who consider themselves "traditional" or "progressive."

Table 18: **"Traditional" and "Progressive" Parents Agreement with Church Teaching**

	Strongly Agree	Neutral	Strongly Disagree	Don't Know/ Understand
Birth Control-				
(very)Traditional				
(n = 31)	11 (35%)	7 (23%)	13 (42%)	0
(very)Progressive				
(n = 120)	9 (7%)	11(9%)	98 (82%)	2 (2%)
Masturbation-				
(very)Traditional				
(n = 30)	12 (40%)	6 (20%)	7 (23%)	5 (17%)
(very)Progressive				
(n = 119)	8 (7%)	23(19%)	62 (52%)	26 (22%)
Primacy of Conscience-				
(very) Traditional				
(n = 29)	19 (66%)	4 (14%)	0	6 (20%)
(very)Progressive				
(n = 117)	71 (61%)	4 (3%)	9 (8%)	33 (28%)
Social Justice-				
(very) Traditional				
(n = 29)	21 (72%)	2 (7%)	2 (7%)	4 (14%)
(very)Progressive				
(n = 117)	84 (72%)	8 (7%)	5 (4%)	20 (17%)

The Bible

When asked if they read the bible, parents responded as shown in Table 19.

Table 19: **How Often Respondents Read the Bible** (n= 200)

Never	Rarely	Sometimes	Often
29 (15%)	40 (20%)	78 (39%)	53 (27%)

Parents were then asked to identify biblical stories or passages that were either helpful, or hurtful or confusing in relation to their homosexual child. Eighty-six respondents cited positive passages or stories. Of those, 47 (55%), cited passages which talk of the importance of love. For example, respondents mentioned the Beatitudes (Matthew 5:3-12; Luke 6: 20-23, 24-26); Jesus' charge to "love one another" (John 15:17); Paul's treatise on love (1 Corinthians 13); and the description of God as love (1 John 4). Twenty-seven (31%) of the respondents who answered this question mentioned the inclusive nature of God's love; that is, that we are *all* God's children created from the goodness of God and made in the "image and likeness of God" (Genesis 1:26-27). Many of the respondents who talked of the messages of love in the bible referred to God's love for *all* (many emphasized all) people and our responsibility to love in return. Sixteen (19%) noted Jesus' proscription against judging others, for example, in the story of the woman caught in adultery, when Jesus says to the angry onlookers "Whoever is without sin, cast the first stone" (John 8: 3-11). Twelve (14%) spoke of God's forgiveness, sometimes mentioning the story of the Prodigal Son,(Luke 15: 11-32) as an illustration.

Next, parents were asked about bible passages or stories that were hurtful or confusing in relation to their homosexual child. Again, there were 86 responses. In general the responses could be grouped into five categories: twenty-four (28%) said Leviticus 18:22, 20:13; twenty-two (26%) noted the Sodom and Gomorrah story (Genesis 19: 1-1); twenty-two (26%) recalled generally negative phrases from the bible, or comments from others to that effect; nineteen (22%) noted an appreciation for the historical and social context of a passage or story, indicating that perhaps some of the passages usually thought of as negative might have a different interpretation; and sixteen (19%) mentioned some of the writings of Paul as being problematic, seven specifically citing Romans 1:26-27.

The Catholic Church

Questions 36 and 37 asked parents the same questions about their Catholic faith: what in their Catholic faith was helpful, or hurtful or confusing, in relation to their homosexual child (see Table 20).

Table 20: **What Parents Found Helpful in Their Catholic Faith**
(n = 162, respondents could indicate more than one thing)

What was helpful?	Number (%)
God's love and acceptance	69 (43%)
Church teaching: documents, bishops, AOC	43 (27%)
Individual priests & nuns, faith community	39 (24%)
Prayer and Sacraments	14 (9%)
Support Groups, Retreats, Ministries, etc.	11 (7%)

Of the 160 who responded to these questions 69 (43%) said what was helpful in their Catholic faith was knowing of God's "love," "mercy," "compassion," "forgiveness" and "acceptance." Forty-three (27%) found Church teaching helpful, and nine of those mentioned things they had learned from documents such as the *Baltimore Catechism* (1953), paraphrasing passages such as, " God made us to show forth His goodness and to share with us His everlasting happiness in heaven" (Baltimore Catechism, 1953, #3), and "to gain the happiness of heaven we must know, love and serve God in this world" (*Baltimore Catechism*, 1953, #4). Four respondents specified Church teaching on primacy of conscience; and one wrote of Vatican documents, such as *Humanae Vitae* (the 1968 encyclical that reiterated the ban on artificial birth control) and Pope John Paul II's *Veritatis Splendor* (The Splendor of Truth); 14 (9% of total) cited particular Bishops who had been "positive," and "gracious," "compassionate," and "sensitive" to gay and lesbian Catholics and their families. An additional 20 (13%) specifically mentioned *Always Our Children* (AOC) the 1997 pastoral letter from the U.S. Bishops to parents of homosexual children. Thirty-nine (24%) mentioned priests, nuns and their Catholic faith community. Fourteen (9%) said prayer and the sacraments, particularly Baptism and Eucharist, and 11 (7%) noted support groups, retreats, workshops and various parish and diocesan ministries.

What parents found hurtful or confusing about their Catholic faith can be organized into six categories as shown in Table 21.

Parents were most upset with their sense that the church was judging and condemning their gay child, and that such judgment encourages prejudice and discrimination. They noted the "so-called 'faithful' . . . [who are] quick to pass judgment and show prejudice;" and the "outright hostility we are experiencing now in (our diocese) led by our Archbishop;" and "negative preaching," and the teaching that says their child is "disordered" or "defective." They were also concerned about the mandate of lifelong sexual abstinence for their gay child, worried that their child would be condemned to a lonely life. One parent wrote: "Teaching (that) gay people must be celibate is unrealistic, undoable, denies fulfillment of their sexuality . . ." The other four categories: (a) lack of support, (b) silence, (c) confusion and inconsistency, and (d) ignorance or lack of understanding all belong under the general scope of pastoral care.

Table 21: **What Parents Found Hurtful or Confusing in Their Catholic Faith** (n = 160, respondents could indicate more than one thing)

What was hurtful or confusing?	Number (%)
Condemnation, judgment, discrimination, prejudice	85 (56%)
Required celibacy	30 (20%)
Lack of Support	21 (14%)
Silence	20 (13%)
Confusion, inconsistency	16 (10%)
Ignorance, lack of understanding	12 (8%)

To conclude the Religious Framework section, parents were asked if their understanding of church teaching had changed since they first learned their child was gay. Less than half the respondents answered this question and many who did used the space to reiterate their concerns. Themes that recurred through their comments include the following: the comfort and support of *Always Our Children*, a generally better understanding of the full church teaching, including primacy of conscience. Many are still struggling with what they see as inconsistencies in the teaching. One parent wrote: "I can't understand. When I went to Catholic school, I was taught to accept and love everyone. Now I find my church can't accept my son as he is." Some continue to espouse the idea of loving the sinner but hating the sin. And six parents said clearly that they had lost all confidence in the church teaching on this matter: "I do not care what the church teaches regarding homosexuality."

Pastoral Support

This section of the survey examines the support that parents received from the Church at a time of stress in their family. The first set of questions asks parents if their Catholic faith was helpful or an obstacle, if they needed someone to talk to, if they needed accurate information about homosexuality and about related church teaching. The end of this set asks if the parent still feels the need for support and information, and how important is it to them to get that from the Catholic Church (see Table 22).

Table 22: **Respondents' assessment of need for, and availability of, support and information . . . from the Church**

	Very Much				Not at all
	1	2	3	4	5
Was Catholic faith helpful? (n = 194)	67 (35%)	25 (13%)	38 (20%)	20 (10%)	44 (23%)
Was Catholic faith obstacle? (n = 192)	31 (16%)	29 (15%)	36 (19%)	25 (13%)	71 (37%)
Did you need support? (n = 201)	123 (61%)	27 (13%)	23 (11%)	12 (6%)	16 (8%)
Did you need information about homosexuality? (n = 201)	131 (65%)	22 (11%)	23 (11%)	9 (4%)	16 (8%)
Did you need information about Church teaching? (n = 200)	88 (44%)	28 (14%)	35 (18%)	18 (9%)	31 (15%)
Do you still feel the need for support? (n = 202)	64 (32%)	45 (22%)	33 (16%)	31 (15%)	29 (14%)
How important to get that support and information from the Church? (n = 195)	81 (41%)	43 (22%)	28 (14%)	17 (9%)	26 (13%)

When asked if they had approached a priest, nun or pastoral counselor for help, parents answered as shown in Table 23.

Table 23: **Helpfulness of Religious Professional Approached by Respondents**

Approached	Very Helpful				No help at all
	1	2	3	4	5
Priest	67	15	14	7	23
n = 126	(53%)	(12%)	(11%)	(3%)	(18%)
Religious Sister	36	4	3	0	1
n = 44	(82%)	(9%)	(7%)	0	(2%)
Pastoral Counselor	19	4	1	3	2
n = 29	(66%)	(14%)	(3%)	(10%)	(7%)

Fifty-eight (28% of total) respondents said they did not approach any of the professionals listed. Those who did avail themselves of such help were asked to comment on how it was or was not helpful. Of the 126 who commented, 74 (59%) said the person they approached was supportive, reassuring, non-judgmental, accepting and comforting; 25 (20%) received helpful information; 25 (20%) were referred to other resources; 15 (12%) said it was most helpful just to know someone was listening; and 32 (25%) felt the encounter was not helpful at all.

What Parents Need From The Church

Of the 114 respondents who sought support someplace other than church ministers, 57 (50%) found support at PFLAG (Parents Families and Friends of Lesbians and Gays) meetings. Others turned to friends, family members, gay people they knew, gay/lesbian resources in their area, and professional counselors. Parents were then asked how the church could be more helpful (see Table 24).

Table 24: **What Respondents Said They Need From the Church**
(n = 148, respondents could note more than one need)

What parents need from the Church	Number (%)
A welcoming environment	57 (34%)
Support groups, networking for parents	53 (32%)
Affirmation and reassurance	39 (23%)
Education - for the whole faith community from pastor to person in pew	36 (22%)

Four areas of need were found among the responses. *First*, there is a need for parishes to create a welcoming environment for gay and lesbian Catholics and their families. One said, "Welcome homosexual people to be active participants in church." Another said, "The silence must be broken. . . . Parents of gay and lesbian people need to hear them mentioned in prayer." *Second*, a need for support groups for parents, or a network of people who could share their experiences and encourage each other. *Third*, affirmation of parents' love for their child and assurance that their gay child is loved by God. "Assure us that our child is a child of God and should be included in the faith community." Another said, "[Don't be] afraid or too embarrassed to talk about this; [be] more welcoming to parents, don't put them 'in the closet' also." *Finally*, parents see a need for education, for everyone from the pastor and parish staff to the people in the pew.

Reactions to Always Our Children

Parents were asked if they had read *Always Our Children, A Pastoral Message to Parents of Homosexual Children and Suggestions for Pastoral Ministers* (Question 44), and if they thought it would be helpful to other parents (Question 44a). Of the 191 responding to Question 44, 136 (71%) had read the document. Only 128 respondents answered Question 44a. Of those, 123 (96%) thought it would be helpful to other parents, and 5 (4%) did not. Respondents were encouraged to comment on its helpfulness or lack thereof.

Sixty-four persons (66%) of those commenting on the document expressed support for it. For example: "It validates our love for our child," "It tells parents that 'love' is greater than any institution—church or otherwise," "It gives parents hope for a better life for their children," and " It expresses justice and compassion for homosexuals." However, 39% of those who support the document qualified their support. For example: "It is a very small step," "[It] neglects the role of conscience," "[It] needs to be stronger, more affirmative," and several said, "It doesn't go far enough."

Another 16% (16) focused on their own assessment of the shortcomings of the document. These comments ran along the lines of "too little, too late," and a general sense that the expectation of lifelong celibacy was unrealistic and would mean a lonely life for their child. Finally, 14% expressed concern that the document would not be disseminated or implemented on the diocesan or parish level. One parent wrote: "Yes I think it can help, but I don't think many parents will read it. The bishops put this pastoral message out and they think it is enough. There won't be much dialogue on it." Another parent said, "I think it has already been put aside by most bishops."

Changes in Attitudes

The survey concludes with three questions asking the parents if they have experienced any change in attitude since learning of their child's homosexual orientation. First, parents were asked to assess their own comfort level in relation to their gay child. Most parents reported being very comfortable (see Table 25). Then they were asked if their relationship with their gay child had changed, and if their religious beliefs had been instrumental in that change (see Table 26).

Table 25: **How Comfortable Are Parents With People Knowing They Have a Gay Child?** (n = 191)

	Very Comfortable				Very Uncomfortable
Comfort Level	1	2	3	4	5
Number (%)	60	42	51	17	21
	(31%)	(22%)	(27 %)	(9%)	(11%)

Table 26: **Has Relationship With Gay Child Changed, and We re Religious Beliefs Instrumental in That Change?**

	Yes	No
Has Relationship Changed? (n = 191)	131 (69%)	60 (31%)
Were Religious Beliefs Instrumental in the Change? (n = 127)	81 (53%)	71 (47%)

A further breakdown based on the accompanying comments shows that 120 (92% of those answering this question; 57% of total responses) of the changes were for the better and 11 (8%) were changes for the worse. Of those who said there was a change for the better, 52 used very clear statements, such as: "We have become closer than before," and "Our relationship (son's and mine) has deepened." When answering if religious beliefs played a part in the change, the difference was not so great. Many who commented made a distinction between their faith as Christian and their adherence to church teaching. For example: ". . .my acceptance seemed to go against my understanding of Church teaching—not my understanding of being Christian," and [What has been instrumental is] my belief in God rather than church's teachings; my belief in Jesus' acceptance of all; my belief in his universal love."

Summary

This survey provided numerical data and comments by Catholic parents of gay sons and lesbian daughters that can provide information to those who work in ministry with gay and lesbian Catholics and their parents. The respondents shared their feelings and attitudes about their gay children and their faith. They indicated some of their needs and suggested some actions to meet those needs.

Appendix C: Groups Participating in the Survey – and Others

Listed below are the groups, associations, and organizations contacted in the process of implementing the survey. Those who actually participated by allowing distribution of the survey to their members are indicated by an *. Other groups are listed at the end.

*Catholic Gay and Lesbian Family Ministry (CG&LFM). Founded in 1992, CG&LFM is based in Rochester, New York. CG&LFM advocates for pastoral care for gay and lesbian Catholics and their families on behalf of the Diocese of Rochester, NY. CGLFM provides educational forums for parishes and other church-related groups, and offers an annual day of reflection for parents. Contact: Casey & Mary Ellen Lopata, P.O. Box 18271, Rochester, NY 14620; phone: 585.271.7363; email: cglfm@aol.com.

*Catholic Parents Network (CPN). CPN is an association of Catholic parents of gay or lesbian children and a project of **New Ways Ministry. (NOTE: New Ways Ministry, founded in 1977, is a national Catholic research, reflection and resource center providing a bridge-building ministry of reconciliation for gay and lesbian persons, their families and friends, and the Catholic Church.)** CPN offers support and resources for parents in various stages of facing the reality of having a gay son or lesbian daughter. Though not a membership organization, it maintains a confidential mailing list of interested Catholic parents. CPN offers weekend retreats throughout the United States. In some areas of the country individual parents have facilitated Catholic support groups for parents under the name Catholic Parents Network. Contact: New Ways Ministry, 4012 29th Street, Mt. Rainier, MD 20712; phone: 301.277.5674; email: newways@juno.com; website:www.newwaysministry.org.

Courage/EnCourage. These are respectively "two spiritual support groups helping Catholic men and women—and their families—to live in accordance with the Catholic Church's pastoral teaching on homosexuality." Courage is for homosexual persons, EnCourage for parents of homosexual persons. Courage was founded in 1980. There are over 29 Courage and EnCourage chapters throughout the U.S. and Canada. (NOTE: Fr. John Harvey, Director of Courage, denied permission to send the survey to EnCourage parents or Courage chapters.) Contact: St. Michael's Rectory, 424 W. 34th St., New York, NY 10001; phone: 212.421.0426; website: www.couragerc.net.

*Dignity/USA. "Founded in 1969, Dignity is the nation's oldest and largest organization of gay, lesbian, bisexual, and transgendered Catholics, families and friends. Dignity works for education and the reform of the Church's teachings and pastoral practices toward sexual minorities and for acceptance of all people as full members of the Church." There are approximately 70 Dignity chapters in the U.S. Contact: Dignity/USA, 1500 Massachusetts Ave., NW, Suite 11, Washington, DC 20005; phone: 1-800-877-8797; website: www.dignityusa.org.

*National Association of Catholic Diocesan Lesbian and Gay Ministries (NACDLGM) Founded in 1994 NACDLGM's purpose is to: foster ministry with lesbian and gay Catholics, their families and friends; serve as a network of communication among diocesan leaders; provide educational resources and models of ministry existing in various areas; encourage the participation of lesbian and gay Catholics within the Church; and to communicate with national Catholic organizations, especially the United States Conference of Catholic Bishops. Contact: NACDLGM, 5245 College Avenue, Suite 310, Oakland, CA 94618; phone: 510.465.9344; email:nacdlgm@aol.com; website: www.nacdlgm.org.

Other Groups

Non-religious

Parents Families and Friends of Lesbians and Gays (PFLAG)

PFLAG is an international organization which "promotes the health and well-being of gay, lesbian, bisexual and transgendered persons, their families and friends through: support to cope with an adverse society; education to enlighten an ill-informed public; and advocacy, to end discrimination and to secure equal civil rights." Contact: PFLAG, 1726 M Street, NW, suite 400, Washington, DC 20036; phone: 202.467.8180; website: www.pflag.org.

Religious

Affirming Congregation Programme (United Church of Canada)
P.O. Box 333, station Q
Toronto, Ontario
Canada M4T 2M5
416-466-1489
www.affirmunited.ca

Integrity USA (Episcopalian)
1718 PM Box 148
Washington, DC 20036
1-800-462-9498
www.integrityusa.org

More Light Presbyterians (PCUSA)
369 Montezuma Ave. PMB #447
Santa Fe, NM 87501-2626
505-820-7082
www.mlp.org

Open & Affirming Ministries (Disciples of Christ)
P.O. Box 44400
Indianapolis, IN 46244
941/728-8833
www.sacredplaces.com/glad

Open and Affirming Program (UCC)
P.O. Box 403
Holden, MA 01520
508-856-9316
www.UCCcoalition.org

Reconciling in Christ Program (Lutheran)
2466 Sharondale Drive
Atlanta, GA 30305
404/266-9615
www.lcna.org.

Welcoming & Affirming Baptists (ABC/USA)
P.O. Box 2596
Attleboro Falls, MA 02763
508-226-1945
www.wabaptists.org

Appendix D: Suggested Resources

Books

Bernstein, Robert. *Straight Parents, Gay Children*. Bernstein's and others' experiences with PFLAG, an organization that helps parents to achieve a fuller understanding and appreciation of human diversity. A call to action to love and accept their gay children, and to speak out on their behalf. (New York: Thunder's Mouth Press, 1995.)

Borhek, Mary. *Coming Out to Parents: A Two-Way Survival Guide for Lesbian Women and Gay Men and Their Parents.* Especially helpful for parents to understand what their children go through and children to understand what their parents go through. (Cleveland, OH: Pilgrim Press, 1993.)

Coleman, Gerald D. *Homosexuality: Catholic Teaching and Pastoral Practice.* Coleman says: "My primary method will be to present information as clearly as possible... to raise questions and to do all of this within the context of the Church's teachings, presuppositions and viewpoints regarding love and the questions of human sexuality." (New York: Paulist Press, 1995.)

Congregation for the Doctrine of the Faith. *On the Pastoral Care of Homosexual Persons.* 1986 (Boston: St. Paul Books and Media.)

Dew, Robb Forman. *The Family Heart: A Memoir of When Our Son Came Out.* With generosity and perception, Robb Dew first takes us into her home and into the heart of her family and then leads us into experiencing how it feels to discover another part of being human. --Gail Goodwin. (New York: Addison-Wesley Press, 1994.)

Fairchild, Betty and Nancy Hayward. *Now That You Know: What Every Parent Should Know About Homosexuality*. If a book can help parents understand what a gay son or daughter is trying to share, this one will. (New York: Harcourt, Brace, Jovanovich, 1989.)

Gramick, Jeannie and Robert Nugent (Eds.). *Voices of Hope. A Collection of Positive Catholic Writings on Gay & Lesbian Issues.* From the Preface: "It is our hope that this resource will arouse and sustain the consciousness of the Catholic community on gay and lesbian issues. May it provide encouragement and support for justice and reconciliation." (New York: Center for Homophobic Education, 1995.)

Griffin, Carolyn, Welch, Marian J. Wirth and Arthur G. Wirth. *Beyond Acceptance: Parents of Lesbians and Gays Talk about Their Experiences.* "Human, poignant description of parents who learn to continue loving their gay and lesbian sons and daughters." (New York: St. Martin's Press, 1986).

Helminiak, Daniel A. *What the Bible* Really *Says About Homosexuality.* "If people would still seek to know outright if gay or lesbian sex is good or evil . . . they will have to look somewhere else for an answer . . . the Bible seems deliberately unconcerned about it." (New Mexico: Alamo Square Press, 2000.)

Jung, Patricia Beattie and Ralph F. Smith. *Heterosexism: An Ethical Challenge.* Challenges the popular conclusion that a heterosexual orientation is better than other expressions of God's intention. (New York: SUNY Press, 1993.)

Kelly, Kevin T. *New Directions in Sexual Ethics: Moral Theology and the Challenge of AIDS.* Kelly brings together the whole of his thinking and experience as a teacher, moral theologian and parish priest, and challenges the thinking of the churches . . . on sex and sexuality as moral issues for our times. (Washington, DC: Geoffrey Chapman, 1998.)

Lopata, Casey (Ed.). *Seeds of Hope: Compassionate Ministry with Gay and Lesbian Catholics and their Families, A Resource Manual* and *More Seeds: A Supplement to Seeds of Hope.* Each volume is a three-ring binder filled with resources to help church ministers study and reflect on church teaching, scripture, the social and physical sciences, and the lived experience of gay and lesbian Catholics and their families. (Rochester, NY: Seeds of Hope Project, 2001-2002. Contact: Casey Lopata at clopata@aol.com, or Seeds of Hope Project, P.O. Box 18271, Rochester, NY 14618.)

Marcus, Eric. *Is It a Choice? Answers to 300 of the Most Frequently Asked Questions About Gays and Lesbians.* An honest, compassionate and comprehensive resource. (San Francisco: Harper Collins, 1993.)

McNaught, Brian. *On Being Gay: Thoughts on Family, Faith and Love.* Intimate and personal reflection of what it means to be gay: whether or not to come out, maintaining family ties, developing an honest relationship with God, building lasting love relationships, accepting oneself as decent and worthy of respect. (New York: St. Martin's Press, 1988.)

McNeill, John. *Taking a Chance on God.* Liberating theology for gay and lesbian people and their lovers, families and friends. Shows that a positive gay identity is compatible with Christian faith. (Boston: Beacon Press, 1988.)

National Conference of Catholic Bishops, Statement of the Bishops' Committee on Marriage and Family. *Always Our Children: A Pastoral Message to Parents of Homosexual Children and Suggestions for Pastoral Ministers.* Pastorally sensitive message to parents. (Washington: USCC, revised 1998.)

Nugent, Robert and Jeannine Gramick. *Building Bridges: Gay and Lesbian Reality and the Catholic Church.* Examines the situation of gay and lesbian people in the Catholic Church today and calls for compassion and reason from those in authority. (Mystic, CT: Twenty-Third Publications, 1992.)

Peddicord, Richard. *Gay & Lesbian Rights.* "Peddicord looks at the personal and social sides of homosexuality, and fairly examines all sides of the Roman Catholic response." -- Lisa Sowle Cahill. (Sheed & Ward, 1996.)

Signorile, Michaelangelo. *Outing Yourself: How to come out as lesbian or gay to you family, friends, and co-workers.* "The stress of coming out will never be as hard on you as the stress of staying in was." Can help parents, siblings and friends understand the fear and pain associated with the closet. (New York: Random House, 1995.)

Shinnick, Maurice. *This Remarkable Gift—Being Gay and Catholic.* Written by a priest, this book combines real-life experiences with a prayerful, faithful analysis of church teaching, especially in light of Vatican II. (St. Leonards, Australia: Allen & Unwin, 1997.)

Siker, Jeffrey (Ed.). *Homosexuality in the Church: Both Sides of the Debate.* Authorities on scripture, tradition, reason, biology, ethics and gendered experience discuss the place of homosexual people in the community of faith. Each perspective is explored by two writers—one more traditional, the other challenging the tradition. (Louisville, KY: Westminster/John Knox, 1994.)

United States Catholic Conference. *Human Sexuality: A Catholic Perspective for Education and Lifelong Learning.* Contains perhaps the most sensitive official summary of church teaching on homosexuality. (Washington, DC: USCC, 1991.)

Audio Tapes

(All available from New Ways Ministry, 4012 29th Street, Mt. Rainier, MD 20712.)

Bridging the Gap: A Theological Debate on Homosexuality & Catholicism. Four hour debate among theologians James P. Hanigan, Duquesne University; Richard A McCormick, S. J., University of Notre Dame; John J. McNeill, author.

Ministry with Families with Gay/Lesbian Members. A presentation by Casey & Mary Ellen Lopata at the New Ways Ministry 4th National Symposium, March 8, 1997, Pittsburgh, PA.

My Brother Dan. Catholic Parents Network. A 1995 talk by Bishop Thomas Gumbleton of the Archdiocese of Detroit at a retreat for parents of gay and lesbian Catholics. He tells of his family's response to their gay son and brother and discusses the pastoral approach of the Church.

Pastoral Care of Lesbian and Gay People. Bishops Matthew Clark and Thomas Gumbleton, New Ways Ministry Symposium, 1997. Bishop Clark urges the church to foster questioning, research and pastoral exploration. Bishop Gumbleton urges all to come out, especially bishops and priests—so the church may change.

Video Tapes

On Being Gay. A two-part conversation with Brian McNaught. Part one, looking at the unique experience of growing up gay, dispels common misconceptions. In part two McNaught shares his own experience growing up gay in the Midwest. Current biblical analysis of homosexuality is also examined. (TRB Productions, 1986. VHS, 80 min)

Straight from the Heart. An Academy Award nominated documentary, this film shows PFLAG families telling their stories with emotion, thoughtfulness, credibility, and humor. (Available through PFLAG.)

Pamphlets and Booklets

Always Our Children
National Conference of Catholic Bishops, Committee on Marriage and Family
Order from:
USCC Publishing Services
Publishing Services
3211 Fourth Street, NE
Washington, DC 20017-1194
Phone: 800-235-8722
         202-722-8716
(Approximately $1.20 each, depending on number ordered.)

Lesbian and Gay Catholics and the Church
Order from:
The National Association of Catholic Diocesan Lesbian & Gay Ministries
5245 College Avenue, Suite 310
Oakland, CA 94618
Phone: 510-465-9344
email: NACDLGM@aol.com
(Shipping charges only)

Catholic Update
What the Church Teaches About Homosexuality
by Richard Sparks, C.S.P.
Order from:
St. Anthony Messenger Press
1615 Republic Street
Cincinnati, OH 45210
Phone: 800-488-0488
Web site: www.AmericanCatholic.org
(Approximately $.35 each, depending on amount ordered.)

Answers to Your Questions about Sexual Orientation and Homosexuality
Available on the web site of the
American Psychological Association
750 First Street, NE
Washington, DC 20002
Phone: 202-336-5700
www.apa.org

Appendix E:
What Do We Tell Our Children?

The United States Catholic Conference says: "Families take many forms and configurations today . . . It is important for diocesan leaders to address various family models in services rendered."[1] They offer these guidelines for areas to include when educating children about human sexuality:

- "Childhood [6 to 11]: sexual orientation".[2]

- "Early Adolescence: simple explanation of church teaching regarding heterosexuality and homosexuality."[3]

- "Adolescence: teaching . . . about heterosexuality and homosexuality from a Catholic perspective."[4]

Here are some ways to apply these guidelines when asked about families with two moms or two dads.

Early Childhood (before age 6): You might say that not all families have a mom and a dad. Give examples of families with a single mom or a single dad, or where a grandmother or grandfather lives with the family. Similarly, some families have two moms or two dads. "It is important for diocesan leaders to address various family models in services rendered."[5]

Childhood (age 6 to 11): You might say that most men fall in love with a woman, and most women fall in love with a man. However, some men fall in love with another man. Some women fall in love with another woman. That's just the way we are. Some of us have a tendency to fall in love with someone of the same sex. Some of us have a tendency to fall in love with someone of the opposite sex. "A homosexual orientation produces a stronger emotional and sexual attraction toward individuals of the same sex, rather than toward those of the opposite sex."[6]

Early Adolescence and Adolescence (age 12 to 16): You might use some of these quotes from various documents.

- "[M]any scientists share the view that sexual orientation is shaped for most people at an early age through complex interactions of biological, psychological and social factors. . . and scientific evidence does not show that conversion therapy works and that it can do more harm than good."[7]

- "God loves every person as a unique individual. Sexual identity helps to define the unique persons we are. One component of our sexual identity is sexual orientation."[8]

- "God does not love someone any less simply because he or she is homosexual."[9]

- "[I]t seems appropriate to understand sexual orientation (heterosexual or homosexual) as a deep-seated dimension of one's personality and to recognize its relative stability in a person."[10]

- "Generally, homosexual orientation is experienced as a given, not as something freely chosen. By itself, therefore, a homosexual orientation cannot be considered sinful, for morality presumes the freedom to choose."[11]

- "Parents and other educators must remain open to the possibility that a particular person, whether adolescent or adult, may be struggling to accept his or her own orientation."[12]

- "The Church teaches that homogenital behavior is objectively immoral, while making the important distinction between this behavior and a homosexual orientation, which is not immoral in itself."[13]

- "It is only in the marital relationship that the use of the sexual faculty can be morally good."[14]

- ["W]e recognize . . . that the practice of many individuals, homosexual and heterosexual, falls short of this norm [sexual genital activity only in marriage], that circumstances strongly alter the nature of cases and that we are wise to leave the judgment of hearts to God who knows all about us, our sin included, and yet continually calls us to deeper life."[15]

- "Humankind looks at appearances; God looks at the heart. [1 Sam 16:7]"[16]

- "The God who is at once truth and love calls the Church to minister to every man, woman and child with the pastoral solicitude of our compassionate Lord."[17]

- "Nothing in the Bible or in Catholic teaching can be used to justify prejudicial or discriminatory attitudes and behaviors."[18]

- "Homosexual [persons], like everyone else, should not suffer from prejudice against their basic human rights. They have a right to respect, friendship, and justice. They should have an active role in the Christian community."[19]

Notes

1   United States Catholic Conference, *Human Sexuality.*Washington, DC: USCC, 1991, p. 88.

2   Ibid, p. 103.

3   Ibid, p. 107.

4   Ibid, p. 112.

5   Ibid, p. 88.

6   Committee on Marriage and Family Life, National Council of Catholic Bishops, *Always Our Children*, 1998, 3rd printing, p. 6.

7   American Psychological Association, *Answers to Your Questions About Sexual Orientation and Homosexuality*, 1993, p. 1.

8   *Always Our Children*, p. 7.

9   *Always Our Children*, p. 7.

10   *Always Our Children*, p. 6.

11   *Always Our Children*, p. 6.

12   *Human Sexuality*, p. 56.

13   *Always Our Children*, p. 8-9.

14   Vatican Congregation for the Doctrine of the Faith, *On the Pastoral Care of Homosexual Persons*, 1986, # 7.

15   Bishop Matthew H. Clark, "We should listen, leave judgment to God" *Catholic Courier*, Rochester, NY, April 24, 1997.

16   Vatican Congregation for the Doctrine of the Faith, *Declaration on Certain Questions Concerning Sexual Ethics*, 1975.

17   *On the Pastoral Care of Homosexual Persons*, # 18.

18   *Always Our Children*, p. 10.

19   National Council of Catholic Bishops, *In Christ Jesus*, 1976, # 52.

Appendix F:
A Pastor's Invitation to a
Parents Support Group

Every week Fr. Ed writes a colum for the Sunday bulletin. In preparation for the launch of a support group for parents of gay sons and lesbian daughters, this is what he wrote in his "Ed Said" column.

Her name was Gloria, and she called one night very distressed, needing to see me as soon as possible. I could tell from her voice that something terribly tragic had occurred in her life. I asked if she wanted to talk on the phone right then, but she was clearly unable to say much more. We agreed to meet the next morning. At 9:00 the next day, Gloria (not her real name) stopped on her way to work. I could see the tension and distress in her eyes. We sat down and she began immediately.

"Over the weekend, my 23-year-old son called and asked if he could stop by and talk with my husband and I about a matter that was very important to him. He had been living away from home after graduating from college and getting his first 'real job.'" Gloria explained that everything in Tim's life seemed to be going very well. He had graduated with honors and was immediately hired by a major firm in the city. They were so proud of him and his accomplishments all through the 16 years of Catholic schooling. After high school they sent him off to a fine college. He was an active member of the parish community and worshipped with his family regularly. That night they could tell that there was something heavy on his heart. They had worked hard on communication as a family over the years. As Gloria and her husband John sat down with them that night, they had a sense that there was something they were about to hear that would change all their lives.

Tim, it was clear, loved his mom and dad very much and relied upon their support and understanding since childhood. That night, Gloria explained, Tim came to tell them that he is gay. He explained that he had not come to this discovery overnight. It was rather, a slowly developing awareness within his heart that he could no longer keep to himself or hide from them. Gloria and John were stunned and shocked. They loved each of their children uniquely and individually. Tim was no exception. He was a wonderful son: bright, sensitive and caring. He had gone through all the adolescent mood swings and idealism that are so familiar to parents. His life seemed to be typical in so many other ways and yet, when he revealed this about himself, an ocean of feelings welled up within them.

After the initial shock, there was confusion and fear, anger, shame, embarrassment; and then a dull sense of being lost came in upon them. They loved their son dearly and wanted the best for him but slowly the implications of their son's homosexual orientation began to sink into their hearts and minds. They began to worry, wonder, and fear for their son.

Gloria came to me for my counsel. She had been in the crowd of many who regarded homosexuality as an evil, a problem, and even a disgrace. She admitted that she was among those who pointed fingers and shook their heads and even felt sorry for parents whose children were similarly burdened.

A flood of questions were in her mind now. How would she and John support their son? What about the church and its teachings? What about his faith? Why did this happen, and who was responsible? What did she and John do wrong that their son turned out this way? She also began to realize that all the accusations that she had made and all the jokes, all the snide comments that she had been part of, were now coming back to point fingers of accusation at her. She was deeply troubled and felt so very alone and confused.

The story of Gloria and John is true. They are two of many, many people I have met who have learned of the sexual orientation of their sons and daughters and have found themselves alone, afraid, and confused. I have worked with many such people over the last 20 years, and I know of their sorrow and their struggle. The sad part for me is that there are so many families who suffer silently this way, have no one to share their grief with, to look for support or understanding; no place to go where they can be helped to understand what the church really teaches and really believes about homosexuality. There are very few places in which they can go and talk about the deep love and care they have for their children and their real concerns about their children's future in a world that so often is afraid of what it doesn't know or understand.

I have come to appreciate how much pain is caused by our quick judgments and easy accusations around an issue that is so painful and so much in need of discussion by parents and families.

We read more and more these days about gay and lesbian awareness today. Our bishops have called us to reach out to those who so often feel excluded from our church community. In an effort to assist families to love their children as Jesus would love them and as God does love them, we are establishing a support group for families who love their gay and lesbian children and who want to support one another. This group will meet soon in our parish. I invite anyone who would like more information about this gathering to please give me a call.